EMPOWERED! LIFE SKILLS FOR TEENS

PROVEN AND STRESS-FREE STRATEGIES TO BUILD CONFIDENCE, ATTAIN INDEPENDENCE, MAKE SMART CHOICES, AND NAVIGATE SOCIAL CHALLENGES

CASEY FOSTER

CONTENTS

INTRODUCTION

This quote rings true throughout life, but even more so when you're a teenager trying to find your place in the world. You're at a point in time when you're striving to figure out who you are and what direction to take. It can be both exciting and confusing, right? No worries—this book is here to empower you and provide the tools you need to navigate this exciting journey with clarity and confidence.

The purpose of this book is simple. It's designed to give you the life skills you need to forge your own path into adulthood. Think of it as your go-to guide for tackling the real-world challenges that may seem daunting right now. Whether you're taking your first steps toward managing your money, learning to communicate effectively, balancing school, home, and friends, or figuring out the best way to overcome stress, the aim is to make these skills feel like second nature.

So what exactly will we cover? We'll dive into topics like boosting your self-confidence and understanding how to make smarter financial decisions. We'll explore how to communicate better with others and manage stress effectively. In addition, we'll cover the importance of trust and empathy in building stronger relationships and explain why setting boundaries is essential. And because we live in a digital age, we'll also discuss being a responsible digital citizen. These are skills that every teen should have to make life that much easier, and you're about to learn them in a fun and engaging way.

Why did I write this book? As I recall my teen years, there were times when I felt overwhelmed by life's challenges and the sheer number of things I had to learn by trial and error. Frankly, my journey to adulthood was a struggle. This led me to write this book: a life skills guide created to help teens. As a teenager, I often got advice from friends and family, and while it was well-meaning, sometimes it was wrong. For example, a grandparent's advice on credit cards was to max them out and each month only pay the minimum due. And I did just that for a time. While buying whatever I wanted started out fun, I quickly found myself buried in debt. I'm sure you've received advice that didn't seem right, but you didn't have a trusted resource to turn to. This book results from a desire to pass on my hard-won insights in a helpful and encouraging way, making your journey less stressful and more enjoyable.

What makes this book different is its approach. We provide every teen with relatable, practical strategies you can apply to your life immediately. In addition, we include real-life examples and exercises to help you build experience and confidence quickly. If you're looking for sensible advice, insights, and strategies to make smarter choices and gain more independence, this book is for you.

As you read through each chapter, you can expect increased self-confidence. You'll become better at making informed decisions and be more prepared for adult responsibilities. Whether managing your time and money, juggling school, family, and friends, or dealing with unwanted peer pressure, you'll handle these situations like a pro. Not only will you begin to trust yourself more, but you'll also actively build trust with others.

This book is organized into chapters, each focusing on a specific life skill. Within each chapter, you'll find helpful exercises, meaningful examples, and real-world scenarios that encourage you to practice what you learn. This way, you get to actively engage with the material and see how it fits into your life.

I encourage you to actively participate in the exercises and reflections throughout this book. It's not just about reading—it's about doing. The more you put into it, the more you'll get out of it. Your personal growth and achievements depend on how much you engage with the content.

As you begin this journey of discovery and growth, remember that empowerment starts with you. I believe you have the ability and strength to shape your future and navigate the challenges of daily life. This book was created to support you every step of the way. Let's start building those life skills together and see where this journey takes you.

CHAPTER 1
BUILDING UNSHAKEABLE CONFIDENCE

Have you ever watched someone walk into a room, and it seemed like they owned the place? You know, the kind of person who exudes confidence like a superhero. It's easy to believe confidence is something you're born with, but that's not the case. Confidence is a skill you can increase over time with practice and patience, just like riding a bike or playing a musical instrument. This chapter focuses on helping you find your inner superhero so you build that unshakeable confidence that allows you to tackle whatever life brings your way.

FROM DOUBT TO DETERMINATION: OVERCOMING SELF-DOUBT

"Doubt kills more dreams than failure ever will."

SUZY KASSEM

Self-doubt is like that annoying, insistent little voice in your head that points out why you can't do something. It's sneaky and always seems to show up at the worst times, like when you're about to raise your hand in class, decide what to wear that day, or try out for a team. The first step in kicking that voice to the curb is recognizing when it's happening. Acknowledging your self-doubt is crucial to overcoming it. Try this: grab a journal (digital or paper) and start recording those pesky negative thoughts whenever they pop up. Ask yourself, "What triggered this feeling?" Is it a tricky math problem, an awkward social situation, or maybe a past mistake you don't want to repeat? By tracking these thoughts and feelings, you can start to see patterns and understand what sets off your self-doubt. It's a lot like detective work, but the mystery you're solving is in your mind.

Once you've got a handle on identifying self-doubt whenever it rears its ugly head, it's time to act. The idea here is to reframe those negative thoughts. Imagine your mind as a radio, and sometimes it's just tuned into the wrong station. You need to switch it to one that's broadcasting positivity and determination. This is where affirmations come in. Take a negative thought like, "I'm not good enough," and flip it to, "I am capable, able to learn, and constantly improving." Admittedly, it feels cheesy at first, but it works surprisingly well. Essentially, you're rewiring your brain to think differently, a process known as cognitive restructuring. In no time, these positive affirmations can and will shift your mindset from doubt to determination, making you feel more empowered and confident that you can stand up to each new challenge (Cullins, n.d.).

Setting goals is a powerful way to help you build confidence. Begin with small and achievable ones. Think of these as stepping stones on your path to confidence. Maybe it's speaking up once during a class discussion or finishing two more chapters of a book you're reading. The goals you create should be realistic and within your reach. Each time you achieve one, check it off the list. It's like depositing a coin in your confidence bank account. These little wins quickly add up and start to change how you see yourself. They prove that you can do it, and that proof translates into confidence (Cullins, n.d.).

Now have fun! Always celebrate your victories, no matter how small they seem to you. Brushing off your successes is easy, but recognizing them is uplifting. Create a reward system for yourself —maybe a favorite snack or specialty coffee, some extra game time, or a night streaming a movie with a friend. Celebrating these wins reinforces the idea that you're making progress and your efforts are paying off. It's like giving yourself a little pat on the back. We all need that now and then.

Interactive Element: *Achievable Goals Checklist*

Let's start with something simple. Grab some paper and create two columns. Title the first column "Day 1 Goals" and the second "Week 1 Goals." In the first column, list four easy things you can accomplish in 24 hours. In the second, write down three more ambitious goals to complete within seven days. Next to each item, draw an empty box you'll check off as you complete it. Once you've checked everything off, it's time to celebrate!

Confidence isn't about being perfect at everything or never feeling self-doubt. It's about moving forward despite those negative feelings and knowing you have the skill set to deal with them. You're building a strong foundation of unshakeable confidence by learning to recognize and reframe your thoughts, setting achievable goals, and celebrating your victories. So go ahead, start tracking those negative thoughts, flip them around, and set your goals. They are achievable! You've got everything you need to unlock that inner superhero.

CONFIDENCE BOOSTERS: EXERCISES TO STEP OUT OF YOUR COMFORT ZONE

Imagine coming face-to-face with a challenge that appears to be out of reach, much like picking up a new sport in gym class. That's what stepping out of your comfort zone feels like—you're unsure of the rules and a little awkward with the equipment but excited to see what you can do once you make the effort. To help you with this, let's set up a week-long challenge to try something new each day. These activities could be as simple as checking out a new hobby, using an app to begin learning a new language, chatting with someone you don't know well, or even volunteering for a role in a group project. Each task should push you slightly beyond what's comfortable, gradually building your confidence. Think of it like leveling up in a game; each new task is a higher level, and with practice and gained experience, you become more adept at facing challenges head-on.

Role-playing scenarios are another useful way to build confidence in social situations. Gather a few friends and create situations where you might have to introduce yourself to a new person or group, present an idea to adults, or even resolve a conflict with a teammate. Verbalizing these scenarios in a supportive environment helps you prepare for real-life situations. You can use these scenarios to evaluate when your emotions may run high. It's like rehearsing for a play, where the stage is life itself. You get to practice your responses, facial expressions, and body language without the pressure of a real audience or conflict. This kind of practice improves your confidence and equips you with the skills to handle unexpected situations gracefully.

Having a peer support system is like having your own squad cheering you on. Use this support as another tool for boosting confidence. Encourage friends to form a group where you can all share your goals and support each other. Organize activities that require collaboration, like a team project or a monthly group volunteer day. This collective effort creates a buffer zone, or safe space, where everyone can push against their boundary walls together. It's like playing on a sports team where you rely on each other, build mutual trust, and celebrate everyone's successes. This type of environment kindles the flame of inspiration and accountability, making it even easier to step out of your comfort zone the next time.

Visualization is a powerful and effective tool that can significantly boost your confidence level. Take a moment to picture yourself succeeding in whatever you're about to begin. Close your eyes and imagine the details: the environment, the people around you, your actions, and the positive outcome. Guided imagery exercises can help you practice visualization. For instance, if you're nervous about giving a presentation, just see yourself speaking clearly and confidently, where the audience appears engaged, sympathetic, and supportive. This mental rehearsal can help make the live experience feel more familiar and less intimidating, like an athlete visualizing their performance before Friday night's game.

We all want to succeed right out of the box, but there are going to be times we fail. When that happens, we often think, what now? Learning from failure is crucial for building resilience. It takes perseverance, hard work, and a willingness to try again. Think of failure as a ladder you can climb rather than a wall that blocks your way. Each misstep gives you a foothold to rise higher and see farther. Whenever you stumble, take a deep breath, remind yourself you tried, and analyze what happened. What went wrong? Is there anything you could have done differently? Is more training needed, different supplies, or more flexibility? This reflection process turns setbacks into valuable lessons. It's like messing up your first selfie attempt and adjusting the angle or lighting until you finally get the perfect shot. Treating failure as an opportunity for growth and maturity makes you more open to taking risks and trying new things. This mindset shift is a key factor in your confidence-building journey.

Together, these exercises are like a toolkit for stepping out of your comfort zone. They encourage you to face new challenges, build and utilize your support group, and learn from setbacks and successes. Whether it's through a friendly challenge, role-playing, or visualizing success, each step builds your confidence in a meaningful way.

SPEAKING UP: FINDING YOUR VOICE IN GROUP SETTINGS

Finding your voice in group settings is like learning to play an instrument. At first, it might feel awkward and intimidating, but with some practice, you can hit the right notes and even enjoy playing. Public speaking, a skill many dread, is a key part of this.

Approach it step by step, simplifying it into smaller, more achievable tasks. Start by crafting a short speech on a topic that inspires you—maybe your favorite singer or movie or an unforgettable trip. Write it out, practice it privately in front of a mirror, and then deliver it to a trusted friend or family member. This safe space lets you experiment without fear of judgment. After your performance, ask for feedback. Remember that giving a friend a proper critique can be hard because of the risk of hurt feelings, so remind them that you honestly want their input. And be willing to return the favor. Constructive criticism from people who care about you will illuminate areas to improve and boost your confidence. These feedback loops are tuning sessions for your voice, helping you refine and enhance your public speaking skillset.

Listening with intention is another crucial aspect of finding your voice. It's not just about hearing words; it's about understanding the speaker's message and responding thoughtfully. Imagine a friend sharing a personal story with you. Instead of planning how to share a similar experience while they're still talking, focus on their words, ask clarifying questions, and show that you're engaged. Most important, put your phone down. Giving them your full attention will not only strengthen your relationship but will also sharpen your communication skills. Engage in interactive listening exercises with friends and family. Have a partner tell a short story, then repeat it back to them. This practice helps you become more present in conversations and opens your eyes to how much you might miss when you're not fully tuned in. Active listening is a two-way street—it builds your confidence while making others feel heard and appreciated.

Being assertive means sharing your thoughts and feelings honestly while considering the feelings of others. It's not about being aggressive but about standing up for yourself, your values, perspectives, and beliefs. Using a respectful tone and maintaining emotions go far in these discussions. Begin by practicing through role-playing exercises. Meet up with friends and create scenarios where you might need to assert yourself, like sharing your thoughts on a group project or negotiating chore schedules at home. Take turns playing different roles and give each other feedback on what worked and what didn't. This exercise will build your confidence, making you more comfortable being assertive in real-life situations. It's like learning a new dance move; the more you practice, the more natural it becomes. The confidence to express yourself clearly and respectfully will empower you in every area of your life.

Even when it comes across as disrespectful, you should still see criticism as an opportunity for growth. Pause, breathe, and suppress the natural urge to respond with sarcasm or anger. We're not talking about people who are intentionally hurtful but those who may have phrased their criticism unintentionally. Instead of taking it personally and letting emotion take over, learn to view it as a chance for improvement. When someone critiques you, ask yourself if there's some truth in their words. If there is, consider how you can use this information to work on self-improvement. Participate in constructive feedback sessions with peers, where each person can share and get feedback in a supportive environment. Focus on scenarios that deal with conflict. This practice helps you respond to criticism calmly and turn it into a tool for growth. The next time you face criticism, think of it like tuning up a playlist—swap out what doesn't work to make everything sound better.

Finding your voice in group settings is about more than just speaking up. It's about listening with intent, expressing yourself clearly, checking your emotions, and using feedback to improve yourself. These skills empower you to engage confidently in any group, whether it's a classroom, a club, or a family gathering. As you build these skills, you'll find that what you say matters, and you have as much right to be heard as anyone.

REFLECT TO SHINE: USING JOURNALING TO TRACK CONFIDENCE GROWTH

Journaling is like having a conversation with yourself, a private space where you can capture your thoughts without judgment. It's an incredible way to reflect on your progress and figure out where you're heading. Start by setting aside a few minutes each day to get your thoughts down, either through an app or on paper. You might wonder where to begin and what to write. If you're stuck, structured prompts are a helpful tool. Think of them as nudges that help you explore your inner world. Ask yourself questions like, "What made me smile?" "Who did I assertively speak with today?" or "What's one thing I learned about myself?" These prompts encourage you to dig deeper into your experiences and emotions, helping you understand yourself better. Over time, this daily practice builds a clearer picture of who you are and where you want to go (Tilly's Life Center, 2022).

As you continue journaling, you'll notice changes in your confidence levels. There will be highs and lows. Documenting these fluctuations keeps you motivated and provides a tangible record of your life experiences. They are a reminder of how far you've come and a motivator for where you're heading. It's like scrolling through your old social media posts and realizing how much you've grown—not just in how you look but in who you are.

Setting intentions through journaling is another powerful self-help tool. Each morning, take a moment to write down one positive intention for the day. Think about what you want to achieve and how you want to feel. Here's an example. "Today, I will approach challenges with a calm and open mind, focusing on progress rather than perfection." This intention can act as a guiding light or reminder, helping you focus your efforts on your goals and aspirations.

Incorporate gratitude into your journaling practice to add even more positivity. Start or end your entries by listing three things you're grateful for. They don't have to be huge—small things can make a big difference in your level of optimism. Maybe it's finding the last piece of pizza still waiting for you, hitting a perfect shot in your favorite game, receiving a compliment on your outfit, or seeing a cute text notification pop up. This practice shifts your focus from what's lacking to what's abundant in your life. It builds resilience and optimism. Gratitude helps you appreciate the present moment, making you more aware of your strengths, opportunities, and blessings.

Journaling isn't just about writing; it's a journey of self-discovery and growth. It's about reflecting on where you've been, where you are, and where you're going. So grab a notebook or open that app, find a quiet spot, and start capturing the words. Whether you're setting intentions, tracking your growth, or expressing gratitude, these practices will illuminate the path to self-confidence and personal development. The written lines from your journal become a multi-layered canvas of your thoughts, dreams, and aspirations, capturing the essence of who you are and hinting at who you're becoming.

EMBRACE YOUR UNIQUENESS: CELEBRATING INDIVIDUALITY

"If you can't love yourself, how in the hell are you gonna love somebody else?"

RUPAUL

These powerful words come from someone who knows all about accepting and celebrating who they are. Embracing what makes you different is like discovering a playlist that's totally your vibe—it's full of unique tracks that no one else has. It makes you stand out in the best way. Are you still figuring out the things you enjoy that make you unique? One way to start this adventure of self-discovery is through personality quizzes and self-assessment tools. Find them online. These are not only fun but incredibly revealing. They help you understand your strengths, preferences, and the areas you may want to strengthen. Think of them as a map guiding you toward your true self. Whether you're an extroverted leader, an introverted gamer, or a thoughtful observer, knowing yourself better can boost your confidence and help you make choices aligned with who you are.

Art and music are powerful avenues for self-expression. They let you showcase your personality in ways words sometimes can't. Whether it's the art of glass fusing, playing an instrument, or writing short stories, these creative outlets allow you to explore and express your feelings and ideas. They are like captions to your life, giving others a glimpse of your thoughts, feelings, and what makes you who you are. Creating something from the heart brings joy and connects you with others who have the same interests, building a sense of belonging and community. So light up that kiln, strum the strings, or bring those characters to life—your creativity can illuminate the world with your unique light.

Understanding and valuing diversity is crucial in today's shrinking world. It's about recognizing the beauty in differences and celebrating them. Discuss cultural diversity and personal identity with friends or in the classroom. There's a world of knowledge to be learned and enjoyed by getting to know someone who grew up in a different country or even a different neighborhood than you. These conversations can broaden your perspective and open your heart to the rich tapestry of human experience. Imagine how dull life would be if we all looked exactly the same, with the same clothes and hair, the same style of dress, and the same height and weight. Nothing that made us stand out. By valuing diversity, you enrich your understanding of others and embrace the diverse aspects of yourself. This inclusive mindset fosters compassion and empathy, enhancing your relationships and social perspective (Rivas-Drake et al., 2014).

Building your personal brand is an exciting way to highlight your unique qualities in social and school settings. It's about showcasing what makes you special and using that to create a positive impression. Start by crafting a 2-3 sentence personal mission statement.

Here's an example. "My mission is to embrace my individuality, stay curious about the world, and always strive to be a kind and supportive friend. I want to grow into the best version of myself while making a positive impact on the people and environment around me."

This statement is like your philosophy, reflecting your values, passions, and goals. It helps you stay focused and aligned with your true self, especially in moments of doubt or uncertainty. Your personal brand isn't about pretending to be someone else; it's about being your true self and showcasing your best qualities to the world.

Sharing your story is a powerful way to inspire others and reinforce your confidence in your individuality. Each life experience, challenge, or victory shapes who you are. By writing and presenting personal narratives, you solidify your confidence and create connections with those who relate to your journey. One of the hardest struggles is to believe that you're alone in what you feel or who you are. You may think you're the only one who has an interest in entomology, cares about religion in your public school, comes from a different country, or identifies as an LGBTQ+ person. Imagine presenting your story in class or at a family gathering. It takes strength to share your interests, values, and personal identity with others. Yet your story could inspire someone going through a similar situation, reminding them they're not alone. If you're not ready, that's okay too. You can be an advocate for those who are prepared to share and stand with them against the bullies and narrow-minded. Sharing your journey boosts your confidence and strengthens your sense of identity and belonging.

Living authentically in a world that sometimes pressures you to conform to the current "acceptable" narrative can be challenging but also incredibly empowering. Embracing and celebrating your individuality means trusting yourself and respecting your unique journey. It's about being proud of who you are, accepting your imperfections, and knowing that your worth isn't defined by anyone else. So, wear your individuality like your favorite pair of sneakers—true to your style and made to stand out. Let it guide you in making decisions and forming connections with others. As you grow and change, remember that your uniqueness is a gift. It enriches your life and the lives of those around you. First and foremost, love yourself and celebrate *you* every day.

CHAPTER 2
FINANCIAL LITERACY FOR YOUR FUTURE

"It's not your salary that makes you rich, it's your spending habits."

CHARLES A. JAFFE

This quote reflects a fundamental truth: your spending should be less than your income, commonly known as living below your means. Money might not be the most exciting topic, but learning how to manage it is one of the most empowering skills you can gain. From creating a budget that works for you to saving for something big, understanding how to handle your finances puts you in control. This chapter will explore practical ways to track your earnings, avoid impulse buys, and set achievable savings goals. Whether it's your first paycheck or the money you've been saving from birthdays and your weekly allowance, mastering these skills will help you make smarter choices and set yourself up for future success.

MONEY MATTERS: UNDERSTANDING THE BASICS OF BUDGETING

Handling money can be tricky, especially if you're new to managing it. But don't worry; we're here to make sense of budgeting and explain how it can help you manage your finances effectively. Budgeting isn't just about keeping track of what you spend; it's a powerful tool that puts you in control of your financial future. A budget is like a GPS for your money. It tells you where your money is currently going and helps you plan where it should go. The purpose of a budget is to make sure you have enough money to cover your needs and earmark some for what you want while also preparing for those unexpected financial surprises. For teens, budgeting can mean the difference between having funds for that concert ticket or being stuck at home because you didn't plan ahead. You may feel you're too young to think about this stuff, but the sooner you start, the richer you'll be. And the best part? Using financial skills wisely opens the door to independence and endless opportunities.

Creating a budget might sound daunting, but it's pretty straightforward. Think of your budget like a pizza—your income is the whole pie, and each slice represents a different expense. Step one is to install a good budgeting app or download a worksheet template. Apps offer cool features that make tracking your finances easy and stress-free. You can set up specific categories for spending, track your progress, and even set mini goals. They're like having a personal money mentor right in your pocket. Whether you choose an app or a worksheet, finding a tool you'll use is key.

Once you select a tool, identify all your possible sources of income: an allowance from your parents, money from a part-time job, birthday funds, or even savings bonds from your eccentric but well-meaning aunt. Once you know how much money you have, it's time to categorize your expenses into needs and wants. Needs are things like food, school supplies, and transportation. Wants are extras like going to the movies with friends, trendy makeup and designer clothes, or the latest game expansions. Note if the expense is monthly, yearly, or a one-time fee. Sorting them this way shows you where your money is going and where you could cut back if you're trying to save up for something special. If you plan to move out soon, creating a mockup budget can help estimate your monthly expenses and determine how much income you'll need.

Budgeting isn't a one-and-done exercise. It's an ongoing process since expenses evolve over time. Just like you adjust your plans when things change, you should also adjust your budget. Maybe you got a raise at your part-time job, or there's a monthly subscription you want to pay for. Whatever the change, reviewing and revising your budget often is helpful—ideally every month. It helps you catch any shifts in your spending or income and adjust accordingly. It might sound like a chore, but consider it a financial health check-up.

Interactive Element: *Budgeting Tools to Explore*

Do an online search or browse the app store on your phone to find options that assist with budgeting. Use ratings and reviews to find one that offers an easy-to-use interface and helpful features that track your expenses. The app should also allow you to categorize spending, set goals, and even alert you when you're close to overspending in a category. Install the program or app and begin using it to manage your finances.

Budgeting is an essential tool, and finding a system that works for you will make money management that much easier. By understanding how much money you have and spend, categorizing your expenses, and adjusting your budget as your needs change, you can take charge of your finances and successfully live below your means. Start small, stay consistent, and watch how budgeting transforms your relationship with money.

SAVINGS CHALLENGES: TURNING SMALL STEPS INTO BIG GAINS

Saving money might not sound particularly thrilling, but the earlier you start, the bigger the impact on your financial future. And that's an exciting prospect. The first thing you need is a savings account. Why? Because it is the safest place for your money, and the financial institution will pay you interest, an Annual Percentage Yield (APY), to keep your funds there. There's a little bit of magic behind saving called compound interest. Picture this: when you save money, you earn interest on it. But with compound interest, you earn money not just on your original savings but also on the interest it's already made. Here's a simplified example. If you save $100 and earn 5% interest annually, you'll have $105 after one year. The following year, you earn interest on $105, not just your original $100. You clearly won't get rich with just that hundred in the bank. The idea is to contribute to your savings account as often as possible. Over time, this will add up. Starting to save when you're young gives your money more time to grow, making your future earnings even larger. Putting your savings in the right financial institution also makes a considerable difference regarding the APY you earn. Ask Google who offers the best savings rates, but pick one that doesn't charge a monthly fee. It's important to note that before age 18, you may need a parent or guardian to co-sign an account for you (Chang, 2023).

Setting savings goals is a great way to make saving money feel more achievable. Goals can be anything from buying a new Apple watch to saving for your first car or even college. Start by setting short-term goals like saving for a concert or a new video game. You can accomplish these things in one or two months, which helps keep you motivated. After achieving these goals, identify some bigger ones. One thing I strongly recommend is creating an emergency fund. Begin with a goal of $100, then push it to $500, then $1000. Having that safety net reduces money stress considerably. Other long-term goals might include a college fund or a trip you want to take after graduation. Write these goals down and keep them somewhere you'll see them often—like on your phone's home screen or taped to the inside of your school locker. Seeing your goals on a regular basis reminds you of the prize and helps keep your savings on track.

To make saving more fun, try participating in savings challenges. One popular option is the 52-week savings challenge. This challenge is simple: save a small amount the first week, then increase it by the same amount each week. For example, start with $1 in the first week, $2 in the second week, $3 in the third, and so on. By the end of a year, you'll have saved over $1,300! It's a gradual way to save that doesn't feel like you're missing out. Another fun challenge is the no-spend weekend. Pick a weekend and commit to not spending any money. Instead, find free activities to enjoy, like hiking, biking, having a movie or gaming marathon at home. These challenges make saving feel less like a chore and more like a game.

Keeping track of your savings progress is key to helping you remain motivated. Just like tracking your workouts or school assignments, seeing your gains can give you a sense of accomplishment. Create a savings goal chart to visualize this. Your budgeting app may have this option, or you can use a spreadsheet on your phone or PC or even colored markers on a whiteboard. Each time you add money and receive interest from the bank, update the chart. Watching your savings grow can be satisfying and encourage you to keep going.

Interactive Element: *Opening Your First Savings Account*

Here's an interactive activity involving a field trip. If you're 18 or older, visit a bank or credit union and open a savings account. If you're under 18, ask your parent or guardian to co-sign for you. Before you go, research institutions that don't require a minimum balance or charge monthly fees. Aim to find one that offers a higher-than-average APY as a reward for your savings. Bring your ID, proof of address, Social Security number (SSN), and some cash for your initial deposit. Once your account is active, you can start one of the savings challenges.

Adding to your savings might not always be easy, especially when there are so many things you want to buy. But remember, every small step you take now builds a strong financial foundation for your future. Whether it's understanding the power of compound interest, setting achievable goals, or participating in fun challenges, these strategies will help you make saving money a habit. That type of healthy habit is a long-term gift to yourself. Savings can give you the freedom to do more of the things you love and expand your dreams.

EARNING AND LEARNING: MANAGING FIRST JOB EARNINGS

Getting your first paycheck is a feel-good moment. It's like opening a gift you've been waiting for, filled with the rewards of your hard work. But before you rush to spend it all, it's important to understand what goes into and comes out of that paycheck. When you receive your pay stub, it's a breakdown of your earnings and deductions. The amount you see at the top is your gross pay, which is the total amount you earned before any deductions. Then come the deductions, which include taxes, contributions to Social Security, and possibly other items like health insurance or retirement contributions. What you're left with after these deductions is your net pay—the actual amount that gets deposited into your bank account. Understanding these components is helpful because you see where your money is going and why you're not taking home the full gross amount.

The first few paychecks, go out and have some fun. You deserve it! After that, let's plan for future earnings. Ready? It's time to allocate your net pay wisely. Blowing all your money each payday is tempting, but consider deliberately dividing your earnings. Doing so will make it easier to reach your financial goals. A popular method to consider is the 50/30/20 rule. This rule suggests allocating 50% of your earnings to needs, 30% to wants, and 20% to savings. For example, if you earn $200 a week, you might spend $100 on needs like transportation and lunches, $60 on wants like new clothes or outings, and save $40. It's worth noting that $40 a week in savings is over $2000 in a year. This proven method helps you balance your responsibilities with fun while also preparing for the future.

Part-time jobs aren't just about earning a paycheck but also fantastic opportunities to develop work skills. Whether you're flipping burgers and asking if they want fries with that, babysitting for the couple down the street, putting roofs on houses (my first summer job), or working in retail, each job teaches you something valuable. You'll learn teamwork by working with others to achieve common goals, communication by interacting with customers, co-workers, and bosses, and the power of good customer service by ensuring people have a positive experience. These skills are like building blocks for your future career, regardless of your chosen field. Approach your job with an open mind and a willingness to learn. Ask questions, seek feedback, and consider volunteering for tasks that challenge your limits and encourage growth. Each experience adds to your skillset and prepares you for more significant opportunities ahead. Want a fatter paycheck? Reliable and trusted employees typically get better shifts, more hours, and bigger raises.

THE ART OF SMART SPENDING: AVOIDING IMPULSE BUYS

Have you ever walked into a store for one thing and walked out with a bag full of stuff you didn't plan on buying? That's impulse buying, and it happens to all of us. Companies invest a lot in advertising and merchandising to encourage this spending. Recognizing what triggers impulse buys is the first step in avoiding them. Emotional triggers are sneaky; stress, boredom, or even a bad day can make spending feel like a quick fix for feeling better. Stores know this and set up their displays to tempt you. Next time you feel the urge to buy something on impulse, pause. Ask yourself, "Am I buying this because I need it or because I want to feel better about something?" Acknowledging the emotion behind the purchase can bring rational thought back into the decision.

Practicing delayed gratification is another effective strategy. It's all about waiting before finalizing a purchase, especially if it's non-essential. Have you heard of the 24-hour rule? If you see something you want to buy, give yourself a whole day to think it over. Adding it to your online cart is okay, but hold off on checkout. More often than not, the initial excitement dissipates, and you realize you didn't want it after all. This waiting period allows you to check your budget and see if the purchase aligns with your financial goals. Rushed purchases, especially big ones, can sometimes lead to regret (Rodrigues, Lopes, & Varela, 2021).

Creating a shopping list might seem downright archaic, but it's one of the best ways to stick to your planned purchases. Before you head out for groceries or clothes shopping, create a list of what you need in your phone's notes app. This list is your roadmap through the aisles, keeping you focused on your intended items. When you feel the urge to add extra stuff to your cart, remember the 24-hour rule. Being disciplined with your spending saves money and minimizes clutter and waste.

Comparing prices and quality before buying is another smart habit to develop. With so many options available, getting caught up in the first thing you see is easy. But a little research can go a long way. Check product reviews and compare prices online to ensure you're receiving the best value for your money. There are websites and apps that make this process easier, showing you different options side by side. They allow you to compare the advantages and disadvantages of each product, helping you make a well-informed decision. It's like being your own personal shopper, ensuring you get the best deal without compromising quality. One last tip for smart shopping is to wait for holiday sales, especially on pricier items. During holidays like Christmas, Thanksgiving, and the 4th of July, stores often offer significant discounts and special prices. If there's no rush, you may as well save that extra money.

Understanding and using these tools and strategies puts you in control of your spending and saving habits. Whether using cutting-edge apps or a trusty old spreadsheet, tracking your expenses helps you see where your money is going and make intentional choices. Take a proactive rather than a reactive approach, and prepare yourself for whatever financial challenges come your way. As you build these habits, you'll gain more confidence in managing your finances, paving the way for security and independence. With these skills, you're not just spending and saving; you're making money work for you, setting the stage for whatever opportunities life holds next.

CHAPTER 3

MASTERING COMMUNICATION

"Most people do not listen with the intent to understand; they listen with the intent to reply."

STEPHEN R. COVEY

These words capture a fundamental challenge in communication—listening. Listening isn't just about hearing words; it's about understanding the meaning behind them. Active listening is an essential skill that can upgrade your conversations, help you connect better with people, and make you stand out as a leader in any group. Unlike passive hearing, active listening involves engaging with the speaker, demonstrating understanding, and providing meaningful feedback. It's about being present in the moment, focusing entirely on the person speaking, and resisting the urge to prepare your response while they're still talking.

LISTEN TO LEAD: DEVELOPING ACTIVE LISTENING SKILLS

An active listener displays several key characteristics. They make eye contact, nod occasionally to give visual cues they're following along, and refrain from interrupting. They ask questions at appropriate times that exhibit interest and clarify understanding. Listening is an active choice, unlike simply hearing, which is a physiological process. It's about wanting to understand the speaker's perspective. Recall a conversation where you felt genuinely heard and understood—that was the power of active listening. Using this vital skill builds trust and demonstrates respect, creating a more meaningful connection between you and the speaker.

To improve your listening skills, practice paraphrasing and summarizing. These techniques ensure you've understood the essence of what's being said. Try this with a friend: after they share a story or opinion, restate what they've said in your own words. It may sound like this. "So you're saying that..." and then give a summary of the main points. It confirms your understanding and shows them you're actively engaged in the exchange. More practice opportunities and helpful hints are in the next section. In group settings, summarizing conversations can be invaluable. It involves restating the main points after a discussion to ensure everyone is on the same page. These practices improve your listening skills and boost your communication skillset, helping you stand out as a valuable contributor in any conversation (StoryCorps, n.d.).

Some common obstacles can hinder effective listening. Awareness and control of these can lead to better communication. Internal distractions, like your thoughts or worries, can pull your attention away from the speaker. To minimize these, practice mindfulness techniques like deep breathing to center yourself before a conversation. Preconceived opinions about the speaker or topic can also hinder your ability to listen openly. Try your best to approach each conversation with an open mind, free from judgment. This mindset allows you to absorb new ideas and perspectives without bias, enriching your understanding and empathy.

Empathy plays a crucial role in active listening. You may wonder about empathy and whether it's the same as sympathy. These words are different, so let's clarify how. Sympathy is feeling *for* someone—acknowledging their pain or hardship, often from a distance. For example, if a friend is sad because they lost a pet, sympathy might be expressed as, "I feel sorry for you." Empathy is feeling *with* someone—putting yourself in their shoes to understand their emotions on a deeper level. So that might be expressed as, "I feel what you feel." We'll dive deeper into empathy in Chapter 6. Empathic listening goes beyond words; it involves recognizing emotions, responding compassionately, and offering support. When people feel understood and validated, they're more likely to trust you and open up, fostering stronger, deeper, and more meaningful connections (Go Moment, n.d.).

Interactive Element: *Paraphrasing and Summarizing Practice*

Grab a partner and take turns sharing stories or opinions on current events. After each story, the listener should paraphrase what they heard, focusing on key points and emotions. Then, summarize the conversation in a few sentences to capture the main ideas. How did you do? This practice sharpens your listening skills and highlights the difference between hearing and truly understanding what's being shared.

Incorporating these listening techniques into your daily interactions can transform the way you communicate and how others receive you. Active listening is a skill that requires practice and patience, but the benefits are immense. It helps you connect with others more deeply, resolve misunderstandings more effectively, and gain insights you might otherwise miss (My Deep Meditation, n.d.). In addition, this is an indispensable leadership quality. By sharpening your listening skills, you enhance your personal growth and become a more empathetic and effective communicator in all areas of life.

THE POWER OF WORDS: CRAFTING EFFECTIVE MESSAGES

Words are like filters on a photo—they can sharpen, soften, or completely change how your message comes across. Choose your words wisely because the wrong ones can hurt someone's feelings, give the wrong impression, or confuse your listener. At the same time, the right words can provide clarity and even open hearts and minds. For instance, saying, "I can't finish this project," might sound negative and limiting, whereas, "I need more time to complete this project," opens up possibilities for solutions and compromise. What about the tone of your message? Imagine you're talking to a group of friends—your tone would typically be casual and friendly. But if you're addressing a teacher, you'd likely adjust your tone to be more respectful and formal. Recognizing when and how to shift your tone helps convey your message more effectively, ensuring it resonates with your audience. Whether tapping out a text, giving a speech, or having a face-to-face conversation, being mindful of your words and tone can make a huge difference.

Making your message clear is an important part of good communication. A well-organized message is like a good outfit. Each piece works together, perfectly fits, and makes a strong impression. Begin by introducing your message's main point or purpose. Next, elaborate on your ideas or provide supporting details. Finally, end with a conclusion that wraps up your message and reinforces the main point. This structure helps your audience follow your thoughts and understand your message without confusion. In written communication, bullet points can make complex information more straightforward by breaking it into smaller, manageable parts, making it easier for readers to understand the key ideas. This method not only enhances comprehension but also helps keep your audience interested.

Tailoring your message to fit your audience is like adjusting the difficulty level in a video game. When it's set just right, everyone feels engaged and connected. Consider your listeners and what their expectations might be. Crafting your message for a formal setting, like a school presentation, requires a different approach than chatting with friends. You'll want to use proper grammar, avoid slang, and maintain a respectful tone in formal settings. Informal messages, on the other hand, can be more relaxed and personal. Adapting your communication style helps ensure your message is clear and well-received by any audience. It shows you understand and value the setting and the people listening, and it helps build stronger connections with others.

Feedback, both given and received, is an integral part of effective communication. Constructive feedback helps you refine your message and improve your communication skills. When providing feedback, focus on specific aspects, like clarity, tone, or structure, rather than making general comments. For example, instead of saying, "Your speech wasn't good," you might say, "I think your speech can be clearer if you add more examples." This type of constructive feedback offers practical suggestions and doesn't discourage the recipient. Receiving well-intentioned feedback with an open mind is equally important. Rather than taking it personally, view it as an opportunity to learn and improve. Constructive feedback can be a valuable tool in crafting more effective messages and becoming a more competent communicator (Le Cunff, 2020).

The power of words lies in their ability to connect us, express our thoughts, and influence others. You enhance your communication skills by choosing words carefully, structuring messages clearly and respectfully, adapting to your audience, and embracing feedback. These skills are about sharing information, creating connections, and improving understanding. As you practice and refine this skillset, you'll find that the way you communicate becomes more impactful and meaningful, creating new opportunities and strengthening relationships.

CONFLICT RESOLUTION: TURNING DISAGREEMENTS INTO OPPORTUNITIES

"Creativity comes from a conflict of ideas."

DONATELLA VERSACE

Conflict might sound like a scary word, but it's actually a normal part of life. Imagine conflict as a bonfire—it can flare up and feel intense, but if managed properly, it provides warmth and light to move forward. Understanding conflict dynamics is crucial because conflicts can take many forms. You might face *inter*personal conflicts, like arguments with friends or family. These are the most common and usually involve disagreements between two or more people. Then there are *intra*personal conflicts, which happen within yourself, like when you're torn between two choices or feelings. Lastly, group conflicts occur within teams or groups, often arising from differing opinions or conflicting goals. Recognizing these types helps you approach each situation with the right mindset. Conflicts aren't just disagreements; they're chances to learn, see things from different perspectives, and work together to find solutions that benefit everyone.

Resolving conflicts involves a few strategic steps. Start by acknowledging the conflict and that there may be emotions involved. It's essential to create a safe space where everyone has a chance to speak but also to feel heard and respected. Active listening plays a key role here, ensuring everyone's perspective is truly understood. Building consensus is the goal in conflict resolution, so identify common ground—what do all parties agree on? Once the issues are apparent, move on to collaborative problem-solving. Meaning, work together to brainstorm possible solutions rather than each person trying to be the winner of the argument. Encourage everyone to share their ideas and consider all options. It's like putting together a puzzle—each piece contributes to the bigger picture. Finding a solution everyone accepts takes patience and compromise, but it's worth it. When all impacted parties feel involved in creating a resolution, they're more likely to stick to it (The Orion School, n.d.).

Role-playing conflict scenarios is an effective way to practice these skills in a controlled environment. As with other role-playing practice sessions, this rehearsal is for real-life situations. Gather your friends and simulate common peer conflicts, like disagreements over a group project or misunderstandings in a social setting. You can also practice teacher-student disputes, where you might have differing opinions on a grade or whether your project meets the assignment guidelines. Role-playing allows you to experiment with different approaches and see what works best. It's a safe space to make and learn from mistakes without consequences. By switching protagonist and antagonist roles, you also gain empathy by seeing the situation from different perspectives, which can help you approach future conflicts with more understanding (LinkedIn, n.d.).

Conflict can arise simply by sharing an opinion. We base our opinions on our unique life experiences, values and beliefs, and perceptions of the information we've heard from those we trust or admire. If you ask others to respect your opinions, return the favor. We can't all agree on every topic under the sun, so sometimes we must agree to disagree, and that's okay. People often have an opinion that will never change, no matter your arguments for or against it. And that can be frustrating, so it's fair to ask the person you disagree with to take that topic off the table in the future. Those who respect you will understand and agree not to bring it up again. Conflicts often happen over topics of high emotion, like religion and politics. When emotions run hot, stop for a moment, take a breath, and change the subject. Don't let your opinion of what is right end a good friendship or relationship with a loved one.

As you navigate conflicts, remember that they're not roadblocks but opportunities for dialogue and compromise. They challenge you to think creatively, communicate clearly, and grow as an individual. Conflict resolution is a valuable life skill that helps you build stronger connections and navigate the complexities of relationships. So next time you face a differing opinion, embrace it as an opportunity to learn and grow. When all else fails, respectfully agree to disagree.

Author's Note

Interested in learning more about this topic? I recommend *Crucial Conversations* by Stephen R. Covey. The book and course are not just for business conversations but also personal ones. This book saved my job during a challenging situation—not because I had read it, but because my manager had. Once the issue was resolved, I read the book and took the associated course so I could use these tools to navigate tough conversations.

BODY LANGUAGE: SPEAKING WITHOUT WORDS

Have you ever noticed how much people can say without uttering a single word? That's the power of body language. Often done subconsciously, it's like an invisible language that everyone speaks, filled with gestures, facial expressions, and postures. Knowing how to interpret these cues can give you a deeper understanding of someone's thoughts or feelings. For instance, a sincere smile can light up a room and convey warmth and friendliness, while crossed arms might suggest someone feels defensive or closed off. It can also come in handy when their words say one thing, but their body language implies another. For example, when they respond that they're fine, even though they look upset and won't make eye contact. Being able to read these signals is like having a secret decoder for human interactions, helping you navigate social situations with greater insight.

Body language doesn't just help us interpret others; it also plays a significant role in how we communicate. Body language reinforces your words, making your messages more straightforward and impactful. Eye contact, for example, is a powerful tool. Imagine talking with a friend; maintaining eye contact signals that you're interested and present. It demonstrates confidence and sincerity, making the listener feel valued and engaged. Similarly, your posture speaks volumes. Standing tall with your shoulders back makes you appear more confident and helps you feel more self-assured. Your communication becomes more effective and genuine when your body sends a message that matches your words.

On the flip side, being aware of negative body language is crucial because certain expressions and postures can unintentionally send the wrong message. For example, avoiding eye contact might suggest you're disinterested or hiding something, even if you're just shy. Similarly, tapping your foot or fidgeting can make you appear anxious or impatient. Closed body positions (i.e., tightly crossed arms and legs) can signal you're not open to the conversation. It's like shutting the door on the vibe of the conversation, making it tougher for others to click with you. Recognizing the message your body language is conveying will allow you to make adjustments consciously so you communicate more effectively (Klein & Madden, 2024).

Mirroring is another fascinating aspect of body language. It involves subtly mimicking the gestures or posture of the person you interact with. It's a natural way of building rapport and creating a sense of connection. When someone leans forward slightly while talking to you, doing the same can make them feel more comfortable and understood, as if you're on the same wavelength. It's like dancing in sync with someone, creating a rhythm that both parties enjoy. However, it's necessary to keep it natural—forced mirroring can come across as insincere or mocking (Van Edwards, 2024).

To become more aware of your body language, try a simple exercise: use your phone or a camera to record yourself during a conversation (with the other party's permission) or presentation. Watch the playback and pay attention to your gestures, posture, and facial expressions. This self-assessment can reveal habits you weren't aware of, allowing you to adjust and improve. It's like holding up a mirror to your communication style, providing valuable insights into how you come across to others. Over time, as you become more conscious of your body language, you'll ensure your communications are more impactful and engaging.

DIGITAL DIALOGUE: COMMUNICATING RESPECTFULLY ONLINE

The way we chat online is different from face-to-face conversations. It can be tricky to convey what you truly mean without nonverbal cues like facial expressions or tone of voice. This lack of visual feedback means our words carry more weight. Emojis and punctuation become helpful tools to clarify your meaning. A simple smiley face can turn a flat message into a friendly one, while double question marks ("??") might make a text seem urgent or even sarcastic. Understanding these nuances helps avoid misunderstandings and ensures your messages are received as you meant them.

Crafting respectful digital messages is essential. The digital world can sometimes make us feel invincible, forgetting there's a real person on the other side of the screen. Respect and clarity should be your go-to rules. Before hitting send, take a moment to read your message. Does it sound respectful? Is it clear? If the recipient stood before you, would you speak to them that way? Emojis can help convey your tone but don't rely solely on them. Words matter, so choose them carefully and avoid all caps because that implies you're yelling. We know punctuation can change the meaning. An exclamation mark can show excitement, but too many can seem over the top. Balance is key to crafting messages that are both clear and respectful (Lohmann, 2015).

Miscommunication is common online, but there are ways to minimize it. Start by being clear and direct with your words. If you're unsure about something, ask clarifying questions. For instance, if a friend says, "Let's meet later," you might ask, "What time works for you?" This back-and-forth helps ensure everyone is on the same page. Confirming details can save you from potential mix-ups. If a message seems off, pause and seek clarification before reacting. Sometimes, it's just a misinterpretation that you can quickly clear up. These strategies keep your conversations flowing and reduce misunderstandings.

Practicing responsible digital citizenship means treating others with kindness and respect, just like you would face-to-face. Be a positive influence online by sharing content that uplifts and informs rather than spreads negativity. Avoid engaging in online arguments, as they often escalate quickly and rarely end well. Offer support or report the behavior if you see someone mistreating another person online. Some groups have moderators that can censure bullying behavior. Remember, your digital actions have real-world consequences. Posting something inappropriate or hurtful can damage relationships and even affect future opportunities. The parents of your new friend may review your FB posts, or a potential boss may do the same. It's essential to think before you post, ensuring your digital footprint reflects who you truly are. Keep in mind that once you post that message or send that picture, it's out there forever.

Online communications may lack the personal touch of face-to-face interaction, but that doesn't mean they have to be any less authentic or respectful. By understanding the nuances, crafting considerate messages, and avoiding miscommunication, you can make your online interactions just as meaningful. Practicing responsible digital citizenship shows that you value yourself and others, creating a positive environment for everyone. Whether you're typing or talking, your words hold power. How you choose to use them will shape your experiences and connections.

CHAPTER 4
TIME MANAGEMENT TACTICS

"Time you enjoy wasting is not wasted time."

MARTHE TROLY-CURTIN

This quote might resonate with you, especially when you're fighting the urge to binge-watch your favorite show or start working on the pile of homework staring you down. But time management isn't about sacrificing all your fun; it's about balancing the must-dos with the want-tos. It's about making time work for you, not against you. This chapter dives into proven strategies to help you beat procrastination, stay focused, and create a space that encourages productivity. Imagine having more time to do the things you love because you've mastered managing the things you need to do.

BEAT PROCRASTINATION: TECHNIQUES FOR STAYING FOCUSED

Procrastination is a familiar foe for many of us. It's like knowing you have a project due, but suddenly cleaning your room seems like the most urgent task in the world. Why do we procrastinate? Often, it's rooted in the fear of failure or feeling overwhelmed by the task. Recognizing these root causes is crucial because, once identified, you can start tackling them head-on. For example, if you procrastinate because a task feels too big, break it into smaller chunks. Identify what makes *you* put things off—boredom or feeling stuck. Once you spot these personal triggers, you're one step closer to overcoming them. Not all procrastination is bad, though. Sometimes, taking a break can recharge your mind and make you more productive. That's where differentiating between productive and unproductive procrastination comes in. A walk or a quick game can be refreshing, but hours spent scrolling through social media? Not so much.

Breaking tasks into tinier steps can make them feel less daunting and easier to start. It's like reading a textbook—one chapter at a time. Start by creating a task breakdown list. If you have a big project due, list each step you need to take to complete it. For example, if you're writing an essay, break it down into choosing a topic, researching, outlining, writing, and editing. To be even more helpful, assign a date to complete each step. This approach makes the task feel more manageable and gives you a clear path to follow. Plus, checking off each step as you go along provides a little dopamine hit, motivating you to keep going. Before you know it, you'll have tackled even the biggest tasks without feeling over-whelmed (Preston, 2022).

Focus techniques like the Pomodoro Technique are game changers for maintaining concentration. This method involves working in short, focused bursts of 25 minutes, followed by a 5-

minute break. Set a timer and dedicate those 25 minutes to just one task. It's like a sprint rather than a marathon, keeping your mind fresh and focused. After four Pomodoros, take a more extended break to recharge. This technique boosts productivity and prevents burnout by ensuring you take regular breaks. It's perfect for those long study sessions where concentration tends to wane. Using an app can help you plan and track your Pomodoros, making it easier to stay disciplined and accountable (Scroggs, n.d.).

Creating an anti-procrastination environment can significantly enhance your focus. Start by decluttering your study area because a clean space leads to a focused mind. Clear away anything that might distract you, including your phone. Keep only the essentials on your desk—like your laptop, books, and a notepad. An organized space makes concentrating on the task at hand easier. If you prefer having your phone present, consider using apps that block distracting content. They help you stay focused by letting you set schedules for when you want to be distraction-free, making it easier to concentrate and maintain your momentum (Preston, 2022).

Interactive Element: *Task Breakdown Chart Exercise*

Take a moment to think about a big task you've been putting off. Grab a piece of paper or open a note on your device. Write down the task at the top, then list every small step you can think of to complete it. Organize these steps in a logical order, and as you complete them, check them off. This exercise breaks down the task and provides a visual progress tracker, motivating you to keep moving forward.

These strategies are your go-to toolkit for taking charge of your time. Understanding why you procrastinate, breaking tasks into smaller steps, using focus techniques, and creating a distraction-free environment can transform how you approach your responsibilities. With practice, you'll accomplish more in less time, leaving room for the activities you genuinely enjoy.

PRIORITIZE LIKE A PRO: SETTING SMART GOALS

Have you ever felt like you have a hundred things to do but no idea where to start? That's where prioritization comes in. It's about figuring out what's most critical and tackling those tasks first. Prioritizing your tasks helps you manage your time more effectively and reduces stress by focusing on what truly matters. A valuable tool for this is the Eisenhower Matrix, which organizes tasks by urgency and importance. Imagine dividing your to-do list into four quadrants: tasks that are urgent and important, important but not urgent, urgent but not important, and neither urgent nor important. This simple method can transform a chaotic list into a clear action plan, making it easier to decide what needs your immediate attention and what can wait (Asana, 2024).

Setting SMART goals is another helpful step in effective time management. SMART stands for Specific, Measurable, Achievable, Relevant, and Time-bound. These five criteria help you create goals that are clear and within reach. For example, instead of saying, "I want to do better in school," a SMART goal would be, "I want to increase my math grade by one letter by the end of the semester by studying an extra hour each week." This goal is specific (math grade), measurable (one letter), achievable (extra hour of study), relevant (improving grades), and time-bound (by the end of the semester). Setting goals using this technique creates a clear path to success, offering a defined target to strive for and a method to measure your progress (Purdue Global, 2022).

To-do lists are classic and effective at organizing your tasks, allowing you to jot them down and check them off as you go. It's satisfying to see your progress laid out before you. For those who prefer using an app, digital task managers are a great option. They let you categorize tasks, set deadlines, and even assign priorities. These tools can remind you of upcoming tasks and help you rearrange your priorities. Keep in mind your school's rules on phones in the classroom, as you may not be able to access the app whenever you need to check or add something. Whether you prefer pen and paper or digital apps, the key is to find a system that works for you and stick with it.

Balancing short-term and long-term goals is like building a puzzle —you work on the pieces before you while keeping the big picture in mind. One strategy is to set aside time each week for planning sessions. During these sessions, review your current tasks and goals, making sure they still align with your long-term aspirations. For instance, if you're aiming for a specific college, ensure your current classes and extracurriculars support that goal. Weekly planning helps you stay on track and allows for adjustments as life changes.

Prioritization means making deliberate decisions about where to direct your time and energy, saying no to distractions, and yes to progress. By setting SMART goals, using effective tools, and balancing your priorities, you can take control of your time and focus on what truly matters—achieving your goals without feeling overwhelmed.

THE DAILY PLANNER: STRUCTURING YOUR DAY FOR SUCCESS

Ever felt like a day just slipped away, leaving you wondering where all your time went? It happens a lot when we leave things to chance. That's where a daily planner comes into play. It's a map for your day, guiding you through each task and activity. Using a planner is like having a personal assistant that keeps you organized. It helps you visualize your daily tasks, making them feel more achievable. Seeing your entire day laid out minimizes stress because you know exactly when and what you need to do. No more last-minute scrambles to complete homework or forgetting about that club meeting. A planner can be your greatest ally in managing time wisely.

Creating an effective daily schedule takes some practice, but it's worth the effort. Start by listing all your responsibilities, from schoolwork to chores and even downtime. Then, allocate specific times for each task. Think of it as building a puzzle where every piece has its place. Don't forget to include buffer time for unexpected events—life can be unpredictable, and having extra time helps you stay calm when things go off course. A sample daily schedule might start with morning routines, school hours, and a dedicated homework session. Don't forget some time for personal interests or exercise in the evening. Including fun activities alongside responsibilities creates balance, ensuring you stay productive without becoming overwhelmed. Consider placing a family schedule on the refrigerator for items that specifically impact others, like if your mom needs to drive you to rehearsal or evenings when you're unavailable to babysit your little brother because you're working on a group project at a friend's house (Vallejo, 2023).

Flexibility plays a vital role in planning, allowing you to adjust to the unexpected. While it's great to have it mapped out, life doesn't always follow the route you marked. Maybe an assignment takes longer than expected, or you get an impromptu invite to see a movie with friends. Being able to swap and adjust items on the fly is beneficial. Techniques like time-blocking let you shift tasks around without messing up your entire schedule. For instance, if you had planned to study from 5 to 6 PM but a friend calls to chat, adjust your study time to later in the evening. This flexibility keeps you on track while allowing you to enjoy unexpected opportunities. Remember, your plan is a guide, not a rigid rulebook.

Regularly reviewing and adjusting your plans helps improve efficiency, so take a few minutes to reflect on what you accomplished. Did you check off each listed item? If not, why? Maybe you underestimated how long a task would take, or perhaps you got distracted. This nightly reflection helps you understand your patterns and pitfalls so you can make better plans in the future. Adjust your schedule based on these insights, moving tasks around or allocating more time. It's like fine-tuning an instrument, ensuring your daily rhythm is smooth and harmonious.

Using a daily planner isn't just about getting more done; it's about creating a structure that supports your goals and well-being. By keeping your planner within reach, you'll find it easier to navigate your day, knowing you have a plan and the flexibility to adapt. This approach not only boosts productivity but also frees up more time for the things you love, making each day more fulfilling and balanced.

FINDING BALANCE: MANAGING SCHOOL AND EXTRACURRICULARS

Finding a balance between school and extracurricular activities can feel like walking a tightrope. Each step requires focus and careful consideration. The first step is evaluating your commitments, both chosen and required. Think about everything you're involved in—clubs, sports, volunteering, part-time jobs—and ask yourself which ones align with your goals and passions. It's easy to get caught up in activities simply because your friends are doing them or because they look good on college applications. But suppose they don't genuinely interest you or contribute to your personal growth. In that case, they might be more of a burden than a benefit. Prioritize activities that ignite your passion or help you develop skills you value. This way, your time becomes an investment in your future, not just a way to hang out with a friend or keep from being bored (Vallejo, 2023).

Once you've identified your key commitments, the next challenge is creating a balanced schedule. Imagine it as a recipe for your week, with the right mix of school, activities, and downtime. Start by jotting down fixed commitments like school hours and essential chores. Then, sprinkle in your extracurriculars. Don't forget to carve out time for rest and relaxation. A sample balanced weekly schedule might include school from 8 AM to 3 PM, club meetings on Tuesday and Thursday afternoons, and practice sessions for a sport on Wednesday and Saturday. Leave evenings free for homework and personal time. By planning this way, you ensure that no single activity monopolizes your time, allowing you to meet all your commitments without feeling over-burdened.

Using your time wisely helps you give attention to everything you feel matters. Time-blocking can be a valuable tool in accomplishing this. Assign specific blocks of time for each task or activity. During these blocks, focus solely on the task at hand. For instance, devote an hour to studying, followed by a half-hour break, and then move on to sports practice. Organizing your time reduces distractions and boosts productivity, creating a structure that keeps you focused and balanced—like building a wall where each task fits perfectly into place (Martins, 2024).

One of your struggles might be figuring out how to handle over-commitment. It's easy to say yes to everything, especially when opportunities are exciting and rewarding. But too many commitments can lead to burnout, stretching you too thin to enjoy anything fully. Learn to say no politely. It might initially feel uncomfortable, but it's a skill like any other. When someone asks you to take on something new, pause and evaluate whether it truly fits your schedule and aligns with your priorities. If it doesn't, it's okay to say, "I appreciate the opportunity, but thanks anyway." Remember, maintaining balance keeps you sane, and it's about quality, not quantity. By focusing on fewer, more meaningful commitments, you can give everything you choose to do your best.

Balancing school and extracurriculars isn't about doing it all; it's about doing what matters most to you. Take the time to evaluate your commitments, design a balanced schedule, allocate time effectively, and understand that saying no is okay. Through this process, you'll discover the satisfaction of skillfully juggling your responsibilities, leaving room to pursue your passions and still have time with friends and family.

TIME FOR YOU: ENSURING PERSONAL TIME AMIDST RESPONSIBILITIES

In the hustle and bustle of daily life, finding time for yourself might seem like a luxury. But personal time is crucial for your mental health and well-being. It's like pressing the reset button on a video game—you need it to refresh and recharge. Scheduling moments for relaxation can significantly reduce stress and increase your happiness. Meditation, breathing exercises, and mindfulness practices are excellent ways to spend this time. They help calm your mind and bring you back to the present moment. Think of it as giving your brain a mini-vacation, allowing you to return to your tasks with renewed energy and focus (Withe, 2024).

Exploring hobbies and interests is another fantastic way to spend your time. Hobbies are not only fun but also promote personal growth and creativity. Whether painting, playing an instrument, or trying a new sport, these activities can enrich your life. They provide a sense of accomplishment and a break from routine. Trying new activities or classes keeps things exciting and helps you discover new passions. You might find a hidden talent while making new friends who share your interests. Plus, engaging in hobbies can boost your confidence and improve your skills. It's like a playground for your mind, where you can explore and create without pressure.

Make personal time a non-negotiable priority by intentionally adding downtime to your weekly schedule. Setting boundaries to protect this personal time is an essential safeguard. It can be easy for obligations to creep in and take over your free time. Start by communicating your needs to friends and family. Let them know when you need time for yourself and why it's important. Ask a trusted person to remind you to pause before taking on new commitments. It might feel awkward initially, but being open about your need for personal time helps others understand and respect it. For instance, if you need an hour after dinner to wind down, let your family know so they can support you. This open communication helps prevent misunderstandings and strengthens your relationships.

Taking personal time isn't selfish—it's essential. Prioritizing relaxation, scheduling downtime, exploring hobbies, and setting boundaries are ways to maintain your well-being. Using these time management skills will make you better prepared to handle your responsibilities while still making time for yourself. As you apply these strategies, you'll discover that effective time management helps with school and activities and contributes to your overall growth and happiness.

CHAPTER 5

STRESS AND EMOTIONAL WELL-BEING

"The greatest weapon against stress is our ability to choose one thought over another."

WILLIAM JAMES

This quote emphasizes our ability to make a conscious choice about how we respond to challenges, which is incredibly empowering when navigating stress. We all face stress, but it's especially common during the teenage years when school, social life, and worrying about the future can feel overwhelming. Sometimes, it feels like there's just too much going on. The good news is that stress doesn't have to dominate your life. By creating mindful moments, you can manage them more effectively and find balance and calm.

MINDFUL MOMENTS: FINDING CALM IN CHAOS

Mindfulness is a powerful tool for anyone dealing with stress. It's all about being fully present in the moment, paying attention to what's happening right now without judgment. Think of mindfulness as hitting pause on the world around you. It's about awareness, acceptance, and patience—not clearing your mind but observing your thoughts without being carried away by them. This practice helps reduce stress and increase focus by grounding you in the present. Scientific research supports its benefits, showing that mindfulness can decrease anxiety and improve mental health. It's like giving your brain a break, allowing it to recharge and refocus.

Breathing exercises are a simple yet effective way to practice mindfulness. They help you calm yourself when you're feeling overwhelmed. The 4-7-8 breathing technique is a great starting point. Inhale quietly through your nose for four seconds, hold your breath for seven seconds, and then breathe out through your mouth for eight seconds. Repeat this cycle a few times. This technique slows your heart rate and calms your nervous system, and you can do it anywhere, whether sitting at your desk or lying in bed. Another helpful exercise is deep belly breathing. Place one hand on your upper chest and the other on your abdomen. Breathe in through the nose, focusing on your tummy rising. Exhale through your mouth, feeling it fall. Repeat as needed. This exercise promotes relaxation and helps reduce stress (Barrell, 2020).

Incorporating mindfulness into daily activities can transform even mundane tasks into opportunities for calm. Mindful walking is one way to do this. As you walk, pay attention to the feeling of your feet meeting the ground, the tempo of your breathing, and the view around you. It's about being fully present in the experience rather than rushing to your destination. Similarly, mindful eating encourages you to enjoy your food, focusing on the flavors and textures of your meal. It's about slowing down and appreciating the moment, which can enhance your enjoyment and help you feel more connected to the world around you. Consciously planning to practice mindfulness while exercising and eating can help make these activities a regular part of your routine (Withe, 2024).

Guided meditation is another effective way to deepen your mindfulness. There are apps offering guided sessions that walk you through meditation exercises step-by-step. These resources are great for beginners and can help you establish a regular meditation routine (Modern Hikes, 2024). Begin with a few minutes each day and gradually extend the duration as you grow more at ease. Meditation trains your mind to focus, helping you stay calm and present during life's challenges.

Interactive Element: *Mindful Breathing Exercise*

Take a few minutes to try the 4-7-8 breathing technique. Find a comfortable spot where you won't be disturbed. Close your eyes and take a deep breath in through your nose for four seconds. Hold your breath for seven seconds, and then exhale slowly through your mouth for eight seconds. Repeat this cycle three times. Notice how you feel before and after. Use this technique whenever you need a quick reset during your day.

STRESS LESS: TECHNIQUES FOR EVERYDAY RELAXATION

Stress feels like an unwanted guest who shows up uninvited and won't leave. It's essential to recognize what triggers your stress to manage it better. For many teens, everyday stressors include homework, exams, social pressures, and extracurricular activities. These elements can create a whirlwind of worry that affects your well-being. Adding a few sentences about stress to your journal can help. Simply note what made you feel stressed throughout your day. Over time, you'll start to notice patterns and can figure out practical ways to handle them. Step number one for reducing the impact stress has on you is understanding your triggers.

When stress builds up, your body feels it too. Progressive Muscle Relaxation (PMR) is a fantastic way to release tension and unwind. This technique involves focusing on one muscle group at a time. Start by finding a comfortable spot to sit or lie down without interruptions. Begin with your toes, tense them for about five seconds, then let them relax for about twenty seconds. Move up through your body—calves, thighs, abdomen, arms—working your way to your head. Each time you relax a muscle group, feel the tension melt away. This practice not only eases physical tension but also brings mental calmness. It gives your body an outlet for releasing stress (Nunez, 2020).

Visualization is another powerful technique to add to your relaxation toolkit. It's like taking a mental vacation without leaving your room. Close your eyes and imagine a peaceful place—a beach, a forest, or wherever you feel most at ease. Picture the details: the sound of waves crashing, the scent of pine trees, or the warmth of sunlight on your skin. Visualization scripts can guide you through this process. Find them online or through an app. They walk you step-by-step through creating a serene mental scene, helping you reduce anxiety and promote a sense of well-being. Think of it as detailed daydreaming that soothes your mind and spirit, offering a break from whatever causes stress (West, 2022).

Active relaxation techniques like yoga and tai chi blend physical movement with mental focus, which is excellent for stress relief. Yoga offers a series of postures and breathing exercises that improve flexibility, strength, and relaxation. Basic poses like Child's Pose and Cat-Cow Stretch are accessible to beginners, and you can practice them at home. These poses help release tension and calm the mind. Find helpful beginner videos online. Tai chi, often described as "meditation in motion," involves gentle, flowing movements that enhance balance and coordination. Short routines, even five minutes, can invigorate your body and mind. Both practices encourage you to focus on breathing and movement to help you stay present and centered.

For those who are religious, prayer and meditation can be spiritually uplifting practices that foster peace and alleviate stress. Reflecting on sacred texts allows individuals to find solace and connect with their beliefs. Reading a religious book and engaging in prayer can provide comfort and a sense of connection to something greater, which helps reduce feelings of stress and anxiety. These practices encourage mindfulness and reflection, promoting inner peace and relaxation in the midst of life's challenges.

These relaxation techniques are practical tools for managing stress more effectively. Whether you prefer journaling, prayer and worship, muscle relaxation, visualization, or physical activities like yoga and Tai chi, the key is to find what works best for you. It's about discovering the techniques that resonate with you and incorporating them into your daily routine. Over time, these practices can help you build resilience against stress, allowing you to navigate life's challenges with greater ease and calmness.

EMOTIONAL INTELLIGENCE: UNDERSTANDING AND MANAGING EMOTIONS

Emotional Intelligence, often referred to as EI, is like having a superpower in your back pocket. It's all about understanding and managing your own emotions, as well as recognizing and influencing the emotions of others. Think of it as the ability to navigate the sometimes choppy waters of your feelings and those of people around you. EI includes several components: self-awareness, self-regulation, motivation, empathy, and social skills. Developing these skills makes you more adept at handling social situations, managing stress, and making thoughtful decisions. In personal contexts, it can lead to better relationships and a more fulfilling life. Socially, it helps you connect with others, build trust, and lead with compassion. It's like having a GPS that guides you through the emotions of your life.

Self-awareness is the cornerstone of EI. It's about being in tune with your emotions, recognizing what you're feeling and why. This awareness allows you to respond thoughtfully rather than react impulsively. Once again, journaling helps, in this case, by building self-awareness. So, write down your emotional responses to daily events in your journal and explore these feelings. Did your heart race when you had to present in class? Or maybe you felt a surge of joy when you aced a test? Over time, you'll notice patterns and identify what triggers different emotions. Knowing your triggers is like having a user manual for your emotions, helping you handle them with greater confidence and control.

Effectively managing your emotions is a key part of EI. It's about staying in control, even when things get tough. Why does this matter? When our emotions go red hot, we often make a bad situation worse. Picture this: you're facing a stressful situation, like an argument with a friend. They say something that upsets you, so you snap back with something hurtful. Your response triggers them to retaliate, and before you know it, a minor disagreement has spiraled into a full-blown fight, leaving both of you feeling angry and hurt. Here's how using EI could have changed the scenario: instead of reacting immediately to what they said that upset you, take a moment to count to ten. This simple pause gives you time to cool down and consider your response. Then, reflect on the possibility of a misunderstanding and ask for clarification. If it is still necessary, share that their comment upsets you. Another technique is emotional labeling. When you feel a surge of emotion, try to identify it. Are you angry, jealous, frustrated, or maybe just tired? Naming the emotion can help you understand and process it, making it easier to move forward. It's like defusing a bomb—once you identify the problem, it's easier to handle it without it blowing up in your face (Ackerman, 2019).

Emotional Intelligence is a powerful tool that can transform how you relate to yourself and others. If you want to be more mature or simply convey maturity to others, master this skill set. You can become more self-aware, empathetic, and emotionally resilient with practice. These skills are applicable in high-pressure situations and everyday interactions, helping you build deeper relationships and lead a more balanced life. As you develop your EI, you'll find that your emotional world becomes less chaotic and more of a supportive environment where you can thrive and lead by example.

BUILD YOUR ZEN ZONE: CREATING A PERSONAL RELAXATION SPACE

Imagine having a special place just for yourself, a spot where you can unwind and escape the noise and chaos of everyday life. Creating your personal relaxation space, or Zen Zone, is like designing a sanctuary that reflects your personality and needs. Start by choosing a quiet, comfortable location in your home. It could be a cozy corner of your bedroom, a nook in the living room, or even a small space in the backyard. The key is to find an area to retreat from noise and distractions, allowing you to focus on relaxation and mindfulness.

Next, think about the colors and scents that make you feel calm and at ease. Get permission to paint the walls or add a big, comfortable chair or pillow. Perhaps a meaningful work of art or lush plant. Soft lighting options like fairy lights or candles can create a warm, cozy glow, perfect for unwinding. Finally, consider the scent of your space to facilitate a calming effect. With the right colors, lights, and scents, your personal Zen Zone will be an inviting and comforting atmosphere that encourages you to slow down and recharge.

Maintaining your relaxation space is just as important as creating it. A cluttered space can lead to a cluttered mind, so keep your Zen Zone clean and organized. Regularly declutter the area, removing anything that doesn't belong or disrupts the tranquility. This practice keeps your space looking great and ensures that it's ready for use. By maintaining your Zen Zone, you keep it as a sanctuary for when you need it most (Foster, 2024).

A dedicated relaxation space can make a huge difference in how you manage stress and recharge your energy. It's an area that's all about you and your well-being, designed to help you rest, reflect, and rejuvenate. Whether you're meditating, reading, or sitting quietly, your Zen Zone is there to support you.

THE POWER OF POSITIVITY: CULTIVATING A RESILIENT MINDSET

Imagine waking up each morning with a mindset that helps you see the good in just about every situation. That's the magic of positive thinking. It's not about ignoring the challenges or pretending everything is perfect. Instead, it's about focusing on silver linings and looking for any positives that help you recover from setbacks. Focusing on what's going well triggers the release of feel-good chemicals in your brain, intensifying your spirit and resilience. This shift in focus can make a huge difference in handling life's ups and downs.

Gratitude is a powerful tool for increasing positivity. It encourages you to notice and appreciate the good things in your life, shifting your focus away from stressors. Adding an entry in your journal for gratitude can be a simple yet effective method for accomplishing this. Each day, write down a few things you're thankful for. They don't have to be big—sometimes, it's the little things like a sunny day or a kind word from a friend. Daily gratitude exercises at the start or end of your day can train your mind to seek out positive experiences. They ground you in the present moment and remind you of what truly matters, promoting a more positive and resilient mindset.

Negative thoughts can sometimes play on repeat in your mind. But with cognitive reframing, you can challenge these negative bias loops and change them. It's about questioning the thoughts that bring you down and looking for a different perspective. Start by identifying cognitive distortions—those sneaky thoughts that aren't entirely true. Maybe it's thinking, "I always mess up," when you just made this mistake once. When you identify these thoughts, practice positive self-talk. Replace the negative thought with something more balanced, like, "I made a mistake, but I can learn from it." Edit the narrative so it supports rather than undermines you. This shift helps you build a more positive internal dialogue (Headspace, n.d.).

Surrounding yourself with supportive and positive people is like creating a safety net for your mental health. Friends and mentors who uplift and encourage you can make a big difference in how you see yourself and your possibilities. Sometimes, you won't see how negative and debilitating a friend is until you meet someone who is the opposite. Building a support network doesn't happen overnight, but there are strategies to connect with positive peers and mentors. Join clubs or groups that share your interests, where you'll likely meet like-minded people. Reach out to teachers or leaders from your place of worship whom you admire for guidance or advice. Engaging with positive influences reinforces your resilience and boosts your confidence, giving you that extra push when needed. It's like having a playlist of hype songs that keeps you motivated and lifts you up when things get tough (Levison, n.d.).

The power of positivity lies in its ability to transform how you experience and respond to life. By understanding positive thinking, practicing gratitude, reframing negative thoughts, and building a supportive network, you cultivate a mindset that not only withstands challenges but overcomes them. This chapter has been about more than just dealing with stress—it's about equipping you with the tools to maintain your well-being and grow stronger. With these skills, you're ready to move forward, no matter what comes next.

YOUR REVIEW WILL MAKE A DIFFERENCE
UNLOCK THE POWER OF POSITIVITY

"No act of kindness, no matter how small, is ever wasted."

AESOP

Did you know that doing something kind—like helping someone by writing a simple review—can brighten their day and yours?

By sharing your thoughts on *Empowered! Life Skills for Teens*, you can help another teen just like you—someone who's ready to grow but might not know where to begin.

My goal is to make life skills fun, easy to understand, and helpful for every teen out there. But to reach more people, I need a hand.

When shoppers browse for books, they often look at reviews to decide which one is worth their time. That's where you come in!

Your review doesn't have to be long or complex—just honest. And believe it or not, it could help the next reader…

- Feel more confident about handling life's challenges
- Learn new ways to reach their goals
- Find the courage to take the first step toward becoming their best self

Leaving a review takes less than a minute, so make your impact.

Simply scan the QR code below to leave your review:

If you've enjoyed *Empowered! Life Skills for Teens*, this is your chance to pass on the positivity! Thank you for being part of this mission to make life brighter for everyone.

With appreciation,

- Casey Foster

CHAPTER 6

NAVIGATING RELATIONSHIPS

"Empathy is about finding echoes of another person in yourself."

MOHSIN HAMID

This quote hits at the heart of what empathy is all about—connecting with others on a deeper level by understanding their feelings. Navigating relationships is a bit like trying to master a new game. At first, you might not know all the nuances, but with practice, you get better, and it becomes more rewarding. Why is empathy so important in relationships? Because it's a skill that helps you build more substantial and meaningful connections with the people around you.

EMPATHY IN ACTION: UNDERSTANDING OTHERS' PERSPECTIVES

Empathy is like a superpower that lets you understand and share the feelings of others. It's about stepping into someone else's shoes and seeing the world through their eyes. It doesn't mean you must agree with them or excuse bad behavior. However, it does mean you can appreciate their viewpoint without changing your opinion or belief. As mentioned in Chapter 3, empathy is different from sympathy, which is more like feeling sorry for someone. While sympathy might keep a distance, empathy closes the gap, allowing you to connect on a more personal level. This connection is essential for nurturing existing friendships, building new ones, and strengthening family relationships. When you genuinely empathize with them, it fortifies your bond, making you feel supported and understood.

Practicing empathy involves exercises and scenarios that encourage you to see the world from another person's perspective. One way to do this is through empathy mapping. Imagine a friend who's going through a tough time—what are they seeing, hearing, and feeling? Write these down to understand their experience better. Another useful method is role-playing differing perspectives in everyday scenarios. For instance, in a disagreement between friends, try switching roles. How does the situation look from the other side? These exercises aren't just games; they're tools that help you better understand the people around you (Wells, 2024).

Active empathy in conversations is about showing that you care and understand in real time. Reflective listening is a technique where you repeat back what someone has said in your own words. It might sound like, "So what you're saying is..." This approach shows you're paying attention and helps clarify any misunderstandings. Acknowledging others' feelings is another key aspect. If a friend is upset, saying something like, "I can see why that would be frustrating," validates their emotions. These skills make your interactions more meaningful and help you become the type of person others feel comfortable confiding in (Hirschfeld, 2024).

Cultivating empathy in daily life is an ongoing process. Add this to your journaling time. Make notes of moments when you felt empathetic or could have been more empathetic. This reflection helps you become more aware of your actions and thoughts. Another powerful way to develop empathy is through community service projects. Volunteering allows you to meet people from different walks of life and see the world from their perspective. Assisting at a local shelter, visiting older adults at the senior center, or participating in neighborhood clean-ups are experiences that enrich your understanding and compassion for others. Your house of worship may have other helpful options. Encourage a friend or family member to join you, especially if this is your first time.

Interactive Element: *Empathy Journal Prompt*

Tonight, take a few minutes to reflect on your day. Write about a moment when you practiced empathy or a situation you wished you had. Consider what you learned from that experience, what you believe the other person felt, and how it made you feel. This practice sharpens your empathic skills and helps you better understand your responses and emotions.

Empathy is a skill that grows with practice and mindfulness. It's about being present in your interactions and consciously trying to understand the people in your life. As you develop this skill, your relationships become richer and more fulfilling. Empathy isn't just a tool for connecting with others; it's a way to create a more compassionate and understanding world.

SETTING BOUNDARIES: SAYING NO WITHOUT GUILT

Setting boundaries might sound like putting up walls, but it's actually about creating space for yourself to thrive. Think of personal boundaries as invisible lines that define what you're comfortable with. These boundaries may include how close someone stands next to you, the topics you're willing to discuss at lunchtime, or how someone speaks to you, and they are entirely yours to define. Boundaries help protect your physical space, emotions, and digital life. Physical boundaries could mean needing personal space or being asked before someone hugs you. Emotional boundaries involve recognizing your feelings and not letting others dismiss them. Digital boundaries are increasingly important, too—deciding when and how you're comfortable engaging online and through your phone. Over time, you may choose to update and redefine your boundaries, and that's perfectly fine—as long as you're the one in control. Sometimes, people might cross the lines you've set without realizing it. If someone constantly interrupts you, disrespects your beliefs, or ignores your personal space, that's a sign they are violating your boundaries. It's important to recognize these signs so you can address them appropriately (Youth Villages, 2023).

Once you've identified your boundaries, the next step is communicating them clearly. It can be tricky, especially if you're worried about offending someone. Setting boundaries is just as much about self-respect as earning respect from others. Using precise phrasing can help you confidently express your needs and communicate your boundaries effectively. For instance, if a friend keeps borrowing your things without asking, you might calmly say, "I appreciate that you like my stuff, but I'd prefer that you ask before using it." Practicing these conversations in a safe environment, like with a trusted friend or family member, can help you gain confidence. Role-playing these scenarios makes it easier to express yourself when faced with an actual situation.

It's natural to feel guilty or uneasy when setting boundaries, especially if you're worried about how others might react. But remember, setting boundaries is a form of self-care, not selfishness. It's about making sure your needs are met so you can be your best self in relationships. To manage feelings of guilt, try reframing boundary-setting as a positive and necessary act for your well-being. It's like putting on your oxygen mask before helping others—you're ensuring you're okay first. Positive self-talk can also be helpful. Remember that saying no is not rude; it's simply a way to honor your limits. For example, if you need alone time, tell yourself, "Taking time for myself is important, and it's okay to say no thanks." There is no guilt in self-care (Youth Villages, 2023).

Once your boundaries are defined and communicated, the challenge is to maintain them consistently. It means reinforcing them when necessary and addressing any violations. If someone keeps pushing your boundaries, calmly remind them of what you've already communicated. You could say, "I've mentioned before that I need my space when I'm upset, so I'd appreciate it if you could give me a little time alone." Standing firm, even if it feels uncomfortable, is crucial so you don't send mixed messages. Consistency shows others that your boundaries are important and non-negotiable. Sometimes, you might need support from trusted adults like a parent or guardian, a religious leader, or a favorite teacher. They can offer guidance and help reinforce your boundaries if you're feeling uncertain. Seeking support from an adult is a sign of strength, not weakness.

Boundaries are about fostering harmony in your relationships while ensuring you feel safe, valued, and respected. They involve recognizing your right to say no and setting your limits, ultimately benefiting you and those around you. Embrace boundary-setting as a skill that grows with practice, and remember that it's okay to adjust them as you learn more about what you need. Each step in establishing and maintaining your boundaries makes you more confident and self-assured, paving the way for healthier and more balanced interactions with others.

TRUST BUILDERS: STRENGTHENING FRIENDSHIPS AND BONDS

"If you have three people in your life that you can trust, you can consider yourself the luckiest person in the whole world."

SELENA GOMEZ

This quote might surprise you, but it's true—many people will be your friend when times are good. A trusted friend, however, stands by you when things get tough, and such friends are rare. Trust is the most crucial component of a friendship, building on elements like reliability, honesty, and consistency. Imagine a friend who always shows up when they say they will, keeps your secrets and doesn't switch up on you depending on who else is around. This consistency makes you feel secure, knowing that they're someone you can count on, confide in, and who accepts the real you. Trust isn't just about big promises; it's in the little things that show you're dependable, like offering a listening ear or remembering important details about each other's lives. These actions create a strong foundation that lets friendships grow and thrive over time. Without trust, friendships are like a glitchy Wi-Fi connection—unreliable and frustrating when you need it most.

Building trust through actions means you need to walk the talk. Keeping promises is a straightforward but powerful way to do this. If you say you'll meet your friend at a particular time or help them with something, follow through. It shows that your word means something, and people can rely on you. Transparency is another crucial aspect. Being honest about your feelings and intentions, even when uncomfortable, fosters trust. Don't recreate the fateful misunderstanding in so many sitcom episodes by lying because that seems easier than sharing the truth. For example, if you agree to join a friend for lunch but need to cancel because you're over-whelmed with schoolwork, be upfront about it. It might be tempting to make up some excuse, but they have earned the right to the truth. Wouldn't you expect the same from them? Your friends will appreciate you being real with them, even if it's not what they want to hear.

Sometimes, trust gets broken, and rebuilding it takes effort and time. When this happens, taking accountability is key. If you've made a mistake or let someone down, express a sincere apology. It means acknowledging what you did wrong, showing genuine remorse, and devising a plan to prevent it from happening again. For instance, if you forgot to include someone in plans, acknowl-edge their feelings and assure them it wasn't intentional. Then, identify what led to them being left out and take steps to ensure it doesn't happen again. Effective apologies aren't just about saying sorry; they're about understanding the impact of your actions on the other person and then demonstrating a commitment to change (Ridley & Crosby, 2023).

Rebuilding damaged trust is a gradual process that requires patience and consistent effort. Start by showing that you're committed to regaining their trust through your actions. Small gestures can go a long way, like checking in regularly or being there when they need you. It's like rebuilding a bridge—each plank you lay down strengthens the connection. Be open to feedback and listen to the other person's needs. This openness creates a safe space where trust can flourish again. Remember, it's not about proving yourself overnight but showing that you're willing to work to make things right.

Trust is vital to any friendship, allowing it to withstand ups and downs. It's built slowly through actions that demonstrate reliability and honesty. When damaged, you can repair trust with sincere apologies and consistent efforts to restore it. Building and maintaining trust in your friendships creates bonds that can last a lifetime, offering support and joy through all of life's adventures. As you navigate your friendships, remember that trust is earned through actions above words, and they're worth all the effort you put into them.

NAVIGATING ROMANTIC RELATIONSHIPS: COMMUNICATION AND RESPECT

Romantic relationships can be wonderful and scary at the same time. They can make you feel like you're navigating an alien landscape or driving a comfortable road you've traveled a thousand times. Although they come in every variety, let's narrow it down a little and discuss those that are healthy and those that are not. At the heart of a healthy relationship are key elements like mutual respect, support, and solid communication. These components create a safe, trusting space where both partners feel appreciated, valued, and heard. Mutual respect means acknowledging each other's feelings, ideas, and boundaries. It's about seeing your partner as an equal and treating them with kindness. Support comes in many forms—whether it's cheering each other on during a big game or being a shoulder to cry on after a tough day. Communication is the essential component that brings everything together. It involves openly discussing your needs and feelings, preventing misunderstandings, and building trust.. It's more than sharing life's big and small moments; it is also about *wanting* to share them with your partner.

In contrast, unhealthy relationships often lack these elements. They might involve disrespect, where one partner belittles or disregards the other, or poor communication, where important issues are left unaddressed and allowed to fester. Thankfully, recognizing the differences between healthy and unhealthy relationships can guide you in making choices that lead to a fulfilling and healthy partnership.

Effective communication in relationships is about more than just talking. It's about genuinely connecting and ensuring both parties feel heard and understood. We put active listening to good use here. Instead of thinking about what you'll say next, your attention should focus on what your partner says. Show that you're engaged by nodding or giving verbal cues like, "I see" or "Go on," making your partner feel appreciated and encouraging open dialogue. Clearly expressing your own needs is also crucial. Instead of expecting your partner to guess what you're thinking, tell them directly. Use "I feel" statements to express an issue or concern without placing blame. For example, say, "I feel upset when plans change at the last minute," instead of, "You always cancel plans." This approach fosters understanding and opens the door to constructive conversations. And never underestimate the power of a sincere apology.

In a romantic relationship, it's easy to get so wrapped up in each other that you forget to nurture your individuality. Maintaining your personal interests and growth is vital, so encourage this behavior in each other. Whether you're passionate about playing guitar, volunteering, or something else, keep pursuing what brings you joy, pushes you to grow, and makes you uniquely you. Having some separate activities doesn't mean you're drifting apart; they're simply opportunities to bring fresh energy and experiences into the relationship. Celebrate your partner's achievements, support their passions, and expect the same in return. This balance fosters a relationship filled with energy and inspiration.

Constructively handling conflicts is a skill that makes a world of difference in romantic relationships. Disagreements are a natural part of being a couple, but how you handle them can strengthen or weaken your bond. Approach conflicts with the mindset that you're on the same side, looking for solutions together. A solution may require compromises from both of you rather than one person getting their way. Avoid letting emotions boil over by taking a deep breath and pausing before reacting. Use conflict resolution skills like staying calm, expressing your feelings without attacking, and listening to your partner's perspective. If tempers start to flare, it's okay to take a break to cool down and revisit the conversation later. It's important to focus on the issue at hand rather than bringing up past grievances. Remember, your intention should be to resolve the disagreement, not to be the winner of the argument. Healthy conflict resolution leads to greater understanding and resilience in your relationship.

Navigating romantic relationships can be hard work, despite what Hallmark movies imply. Still, building on the foundations of mutual respect, effective communication, supporting individuality, and constructive conflict resolution creates the basis for a strong and loving connection.

BREAKING FREE FROM TOXIC TIES: IDENTIFYING AND EXITING TOXIC FRIENDSHIPS

Navigating friendships can sometimes feel like tending a garden—most relationships help you grow, but occasionally, you encounter weeds that choke your growth. There are things you can do if the friendship starts to feel more draining than uplifting. Recognizing toxic relationships requires being aware of certain red flags. Manipulation, for example, might involve a friend constantly expecting you to pay their way or trying to control your actions or decisions, often making you feel guilty or obligated. Exhibiting jealousy of other relationships, your achievements, or that they're not in the spotlight is another red flag. Disrespect can manifest as dismissive comments or hurtful 'jokes' at your expense, constantly being late or not showing up at all, or belittling your feelings and input. If you notice your 'friend' frequently exhibiting these behaviors, it's necessary to acknowledge that this isn't healthy. Toxic friendships can sneak up on you, often leaving you questioning your worth or sanity. They can make you feel responsible and believe that changing yourself might fix everything and restore the friendship to how it used to be. You may neglect positive relationships because all your energy goes toward a toxic person. Remember, a healthy friendship should leave you feeling encouraged and valued, not overwhelmed, stressed, and insecure (WebMD, 2021).

The impact of these toxic ties on your well-being can be profound. You might find yourself emotionally exhausted, constantly on edge, or even doubting your self-worth. Stress becomes a daily companion, and you might feel like you're walking on eggshells to avoid triggering your friend's hostile reactions. Over time, this can take a toll on your mental health, leading to anxiety or depression. Recognizing when a friendship is causing more harm than good is crucial. Understanding the emotional cost of maintaining such relationships can empower you to make healthier choices. It's okay to prioritize your happiness and mental health over a friendship that consistently brings you down.

Exiting a toxic friendship is easier said than done, especially if drama and conflict seem inevitable. Start by gradually disengaging from the relationship. Slowly reduce the time you spend together or take longer to respond to messages. It's about creating space for yourself without abruptly cutting ties, which could lead to unnecessary confrontation. If the situation calls for it, communicate your decision respectfully. You don't need to get into all the details, but you might say something like, "I need some time to focus on myself right now." Keep it simple and honest, focusing on your needs rather than pointing fingers. If they do not respect your wishes and they still won't leave you alone or make you feel threatened, it's essential to seek support. You don't have to face them alone—reach out to a trusted adult for help because your safety and peace of mind are the priority (WebMD, 2021).

Once you've moved on from a toxic friendship, the process of healing and rebuilding your self-esteem begins. First and foremost, if you need it, give yourself more time. Surrounding yourself with positive influences can help immensely. Seek new friends and mentors who uplift and support you, or reconnect with past friends you may have unintentionally lost touch with. These should be people who encourage you and bring out your best. Engaging in activities that promote self-worth, like joining a club or volunteering, can also boost your confidence. These experiences allow you to rediscover your passions and strengths, reminding you of your value outside of any friendship. Building a supportive network of friends and mentors can help fill the void the toxic relationship leaves, offering encouragement and understanding as you heal and grow.

Leaving behind a toxic friendship is a brave step towards prioritizing your well-being. It's about recognizing harmful patterns, making difficult choices, ending the relationship, and then taking the path toward healing. As you navigate these challenges, remember that every step forward strengthens your resilience.

As you navigate the waters of relationships—whether friendships or romantic ties—remember that each connection shapes you in some way. Embrace the people that nourish your soul and learn from those that don't. With these skills and insights, you're well-equipped to create and maintain healthier, happier, and more fulfilling connections.

CHAPTER 7

DIGITAL CITIZENSHIP

"With great power comes great responsibility."

PETER PARKER

You might recognize this iconic line from Spider-Man, and it's just as true in the digital world. The internet offers a vast playground for creativity, connection, and expression. But just like Peter learned about his powers, navigating this space with responsibility and respect is essential. Welcome to the world of digital citizenship, where how you communicate online can shape your reputation, relationships, and even future opportunities.

ONLINE ETIQUETTE: NAVIGATING THE DIGITAL WORLD WITH RESPECT

Understanding digital etiquette is like learning the rules of a new sport. You wouldn't barge onto a soccer field without knowing how to play, right? Similarly, online etiquette involves knowing how to interact respectfully and effectively in digital spaces. At its core, digital etiquette is about treating others online as if you were face-to-face. They are people, and the Golden Rule applies. This principle is crucial because it's too easy to belittle and bully a faceless entity. In text-based communications, the lack of body language and vocal tone can easily cause misunderstandings, making respectful language and word choice even more critical. For example, using all caps in a message can come across as shouting, while excessive punctuation might seem aggressive. Carefully choosing your words shows thoughtfulness and helps ensure the readers of your message understand it just as you intended (Lohmann, 2015).

Communicating effectively online requires clarity. It's not just about what you say but how you say it. Drafting considerate emails or messages is a good first step. Think of an email as a conversation starter: you wouldn't begin talking to someone by shouting or being abrupt. Open with a friendly greeting, clearly state your purpose, and close on a polite note. Emojis can also be helpful because they add emotional context that text alone might lack. A smiley face can soften the tone of a message, making it feel warmer and more approachable. However, use them appropriately and in moderation—too many can seem unprofessional or overwhelming.

Conflicts will happen in the digital world, but handling them with maturity is key. When disagreements arise online, it's easy to dehumanize the other person and let anger take over. How can you counter this? The first step is to take a calming breath. Doing that could prevent you from firing off an angry email or posting to a thread, which you'll likely regret. Consider what the other person is saying and try to see things from their perspective. Are you in the wrong? If so, you should apologize. If that's not the case, and the discussion becomes heated, de-escalate the situation by acknowledging the other person's right to their point of view and expressing your own calmly. Despite good intentions, the best course of action may be to step away from an unproductive back-and-forth argument. Amid a digital conflict, maintain your composure and keep the conversation respectful, or merely choose not to engage.

Role-playing digital scenarios can be a good way to practice these skills. Imagine a simulated social media interaction where a friend misinterprets your post. How would you address it? How would this be different if a stranger misunderstood it? Think about phrasing that clarifies your intent while acknowledging their feelings or ideas. In another scenario, consider an online class discussion group where another student disagrees with your response to the prompt. Practicing how to communicate your ideas while valuing others' input can prepare you for real-life situations. Engaging in these exercises develops the skills needed to navigate digital interactions smoothly.

***

Interactive Element: *Digital Etiquette Role-Playing Exercise*

Gather a group of friends or classmates and role-play different online scenarios. Assign roles such as the initiator of a message, the responder, and the observer. After each interaction, discuss what went well and what could be improved. This exercise helps you practice respectful communication and conflict resolution in a safe environment, building confidence for real life digital interactions.

Digital citizenship is about more than just making use of all this technology; it's about using it wisely and thoughtfully. By mastering online etiquette, you can create positive interactions, avoid misunderstandings while expressing your personality and opinions, and foster a more respectful digital community.

CYBER SAFETY: PROTECTING YOUR PRIVACY ONLINE

Imagine being in your favorite video game, where you have to protect your character from unexpected attacks. Navigating the internet can be like that. While it's a place full of necessary resources and excellent opportunities, it also has some lurking dangers. Protecting your online privacy is crucial because your personal information is valuable to thieves. Here are two common risks you're likely to come across. For starters, phishing scams often disguise themselves as legitimate messages from companies or friends to trick you into giving away your private details. Identity theft is another risk, where someone uses your personal info to pretend to be you, often with serious consequences. Understanding these risks is a major step toward protecting yourself and staying safe online.

Passwords are your first line of defense against criminals trying to access your online accounts, much like the deadbolt on your front door. Creating strong passwords is crucial to keeping these accounts secure. Think of it as crafting a secret code that only you know. To make it complex, use a mix of uppercase and lowercase letters, numbers, and symbols. The longer and more unique, the better. Avoid using easily guessed info or something shared on social media, like your birthdate or pet's name. Consider using a passphrase—a series of random words strung together, which can be easier to remember but hard to crack. Since you should have a unique password for every online account, there's an easier solution: use a password manager program. These powerful tools store and generate complex passwords, so you don't have to remember every single one. It's like having one master key that keeps all your locks secure.

Now, let's talk about privacy settings on social media and other platforms. These settings are like the control panel of your online presence. They allow you to decide what you share and with whom. Depending on your age, these may be controlled by a parent or guardian. For the sake of this chapter, we're going to assume you're in control. Start by reviewing the privacy settings on your favorite apps. Most platforms have a privacy section where you can limit who sees your posts, who can send you messages, and how much personal info is visible. It's like setting up your profile's gatekeeper and deciding who gets access and who doesn't. Go through each option carefully, and don't be shy about setting things to "Friends" or "Only Me" if you're unsure. Remember, the more control you have, the safer you are (Lin, 2023).

Email scams are another online hazard you should watch out for. They're like traps set to catch the unsuspecting. Spotting fake emails is a skill you can develop with practice. A typical red flag is any email that asks for your password or personal information, insists an urgent response is needed, or directs you to click a suspicious link. These emails might look official but often have subtle errors, like weird addresses or poor grammar. If something feels off, it probably is. Before clicking, hover over links to see their actual destination. The safest option is to go directly to the official website instead of following a text or email link. Save important website addresses in your browser favorites. Be particularly careful of email attachments because they may contain viruses or malware. And never share sensitive info over email or text, especially if you didn't initiate the contact.

Locking your devices and logging out of apps are crucial steps to keeping your personal information safe. Think of it as guarding the entrance to your digital world. Log out—even on your personal devices when you're done using an app or website. Doing so prevents others from accessing your accounts, which could lead to embarrassing profile changes, attacks on your friends, or even being locked out of your own account. And don't forget to lock your computer or phone every time you step away, even for a moment. It's like shutting the door to your house when you leave —essential for keeping intruders out. For mobile devices, set up strong passwords or PINs and enable automatic locking when they're idle. Consider turning on features that allow you to erase data remotely if your device is ever lost or stolen. These simple habits create substantial barriers, keeping your digital world more secure.

Navigating the digital landscape can feel daunting, but with the right tools and awareness, you can protect yourself and enjoy all that the online world has to offer. Understanding these privacy risks and proactively safeguarding your information is key to maintaining your online security. It bears repeating: don't click a link or download an attachment if in doubt. Remember, just like in any game, being aware and prepared makes all the difference.

THE IMPACT OF YOUR DIGITAL FOOTPRINT: THINKING BEFORE YOU POST

Each online action you take leaves a trail. This trail is your digital footprint, and it's more significant than you might think. Everything contributes to your online persona, from the photos you share to the posts you like. Think of it like a public record that anyone—friends, teachers, future employers—might see. It goes back to the topic of privacy settings. It can shape how others perceive you, influencing opportunities like college admissions or job applications. Colleges and employers often check candidates' online profiles to get a sense of their character. A single inappropriate post or comment might seem harmless now, but it can have long-lasting effects. It's like graffiti on a wall; it might have seemed cool, but it can leave a mark you might not want later. Being mindful of your digital footprint helps you maintain a positive and professional online presence that reflects the real you (Batchelor, 2021).

Before you hit "post," take a moment to evaluate what you're sharing. Ask yourself a few key questions. Is this appropriate for everyone to see? Could this offend or hurt someone? Would it be okay if someone printed and passed it around at school or work? How would I feel if my parents or teachers saw it? These questions act like a filter, helping you decide what's worth sharing and what's best kept private. Oversharing can lead to unintended consequences, from embarrassing situations to damaging your reputation. For instance, sharing a rant about a teacher might feel satisfying initially. However, if it gets back to them, it could hurt your relationship or even lead to legal consequences.

Another example is if you post each time you argue with your significant other. How does this reflect on you, and what message is it sending to your partner? Real-world examples of oversharing gone wrong are everywhere—people lose jobs and relationships or even face legal issues because they didn't pause and think before posting. Keeping these potential outcomes in mind can guide you in making smarter choices about your online content.

Managing your online presence is like packing for an adventure—you carefully choose what to take to show off your style and leave behind what doesn't fit the journey. Start by reviewing your social media profiles. What do your posts say about you? Aim to showcase the best version of yourself. Share achievements, passions, and positive interactions with friends and family. Use privacy settings to control who sees your content, and remember that public posts can reach a much wider audience than you might expect. By carefully shaping your online identity, you can ensure it reflects who you truly are while staying mindful of how others might perceive it (Batchelor, 2021).

What about removing unwanted content from your digital footprint? It's not always straightforward, but it's possible. Begin by identifying anything that might harm your reputation or personal brand. Include things like old social media posts, embarrassing photos, or anything that no longer reflects who you are. Reach out to friends or family who may have shared these items and politely ask them to take them down. You might need to contact the website administrators for content hosted on websites or forums. Many platforms have specific procedures for requesting content removal, so take the time to read and follow their guidelines. Think of it as tidying up your room; it might take effort, but the result is worth it. While you can erase some things, know that others will remain forever. It's one of the consequences of choosing to participate in the online realm. Keeping your digital footprint in check ensures that your online presence aligns with the person you believe yourself to be, both now and in the future.

BALANCING SCREEN TIME: MAINTAINING REAL-WORLD CONNECTIONS

Imagine your brain feeling like it's wrapped in a fog, your eyes straining after hours of staring at a screen. That's digital fatigue, a typical result of excessive screen time. Too much time glued to screens can lead to headaches, eye strain, and trouble sleeping. Your mental health could also be affected, leading to heightened anxiety and stress as constant notifications keep your mind in overdrive. It's like being stuck in a video game that never pauses, leaving you exhausted and overwhelmed. Recognizing these symptoms is the first step in understanding the impact of too much screen time on your body and mind, and it's something many people experience without even realizing it. If you're experiencing these issues, a digital detox could help. Start by identifying a behavior to change and setting a clear goal, like reducing social media use or avoiding screens before bed. Commit to at least two weeks and lean on family and friends for support (Cleveland Clinic, 2021).

Setting limits on screen time is essential for maintaining balance, and it's easier than you might think. Most devices come with built-in tools to help you monitor your usage. Check out your phone's settings for features that track how much time you spend on each app. Use these insights to set daily limits, like cutting back on social media to an hour a day. Think of it as budgeting your time, just like you would with money. Creating a schedule that includes breaks from screens can keep you refreshed and focused. It's about finding a balance that lets you enjoy your digital world without letting it take over your life. You'll be surprised at how much more time you have for other activities once you set these boundaries (My Kids Vision, n.d.).

Real-world interactions bring a sense of authenticity that is often missing in digital exchanges. They're vital for maintaining meaningful connections with the people around you. Organize offline meetups with friends, like a picnic at a local park or a movie night at someone's house. Joining clubs or sports teams can also be a fantastic way to engage with peers while doing something fun. These activities help strengthen bonds and create memories that no screen can replicate. It's about being present, enjoying the moment, and building relationships that are more than just digital avatars. Prioritizing these face-to-face connections can improve your mood and make you feel more grounded.

Creating screen-free zones or times can help you set healthier boundaries with technology. Doing so fosters more intentional use rather than out of habit. Consider areas like the family dinner table as sacred spaces where screens are off-limits, encouraging everyone to engage in conversation and enjoy each other's company without distractions. You might also designate certain times, like the hour before bed, as screen-free. Why? Because of the effects of blue light. Blue light, which has the shortest wavelength and highest energy in the visible spectrum, can disrupt sleep patterns by affecting the body's production of melatonin, a hormone essential for rest (UC Davis Health, 2022). Constant exposure to blue light may also damage retinal cells and contribute to vision problems over time. By making bedtime screen-free, you not only allow your brain to relax and promote better sleep but also protect your eyes and overall well-being. It's like giving your eyes and mind a mini-vacation every day, letting you recharge and refocus.

Balancing screen time with real-world interactions isn't about cutting out technology entirely. It's about using tech wisely and ensuring it doesn't overshadow the rich experiences life has to offer. By recognizing the effects of excessive screen time, setting limits, prioritizing real-world connections, and creating screen-free spaces or hours of the day, you can enjoy the benefits of doing a digital detox. Make a conscious choice to ensure technology doesn't dominate your life. This balance helps you stay genuinely engaged with your digital and physical worlds, fostering deeper connections and more meaningful experiences beyond the screen.

CHAPTER 8

ADAPTABILITY AND RESILIENCE

"Change is the only constant in life."

HERACLITUS

It may sound like ancient wisdom, but the truth of what this long-dead Greek philosopher said hits home every day. Whether it's moving to a new school, meeting new people, or even facing unexpected challenges, change is always around the corner.

EMBRACING CHANGE: THRIVING THROUGH TRANSITIONS

It may feel unsettling, but understanding that change is a natural part of life can help ease that anxiety. Think about historical shifts, like the evolution of technology. Not that long ago, smartphones didn't even exist, and now they're a part of everyday life. Adapting to these changes has opened up new worlds of communication and learning. AI is another example. It's often in the news because of the advancements we expect it to bring to our lives. Accepting change as a given reduces apprehension and encourages you to embrace it as a chance to grow.

Having a growth mindset is key to viewing change as an opportunity rather than a threat. This mindset is about believing that abilities and intelligence can grow with effort and learning. Many people who have thrived through change have this mindset. Take J.K. Rowling, for example. Before she became a world-famous author, she faced numerous rejections and hardships. Instead of giving up, she saw these challenges as opportunities to improve. You can shift your perspective in similar ways. Try exercises like setting small, achievable goals when facing a change. Each goal you meet builds confidence and reinforces the idea that you can grow through new experiences. Visualizing positive outcomes rather than focusing on potential failures can also help rewire your thinking toward growth (Schwarz, n.d.).

Adaptability is a skill you can build with practice, like adjusting to a new school or making new friends. Start by attempting some new things, like taking an unexpected route to school or picking up a hobby you haven't tried before. These small changes help you get comfortable with larger transitions. You can also practice imagining and thinking about how to handle different situations. This way, you'll feel more prepared when surprises come your way.

Building a strong support system is invaluable during times of change. Friends, family, and mentors can offer guidance, encouragement, and a listening ear when you need it most. Create a list of people you trust and know you can turn to when facing transitions. Sometimes, just talking things through can provide clarity and comfort. Joining clubs or organizations through your house of worship or school is another way to expand your support network. Whether in person or an online community, being part of a group where you share interests can make you feel less alone. When life feels like navigating a storm, your support system is a much-needed anchor (University at Buffalo, n.d.).

Interactive Element: Creating Your Support Network Map

Draw a map of your current support network, starting with you in the center. Include family, friends, teachers, religious leaders, and any groups you're a part of. Use lines to connect people who know each other, and note how each one supports you. This visual can help you see who your go-to supporters are and identify areas where you may want to build more connections.

Embracing change, developing a growth mindset, practicing adaptability, and building support systems are your tools for thriving through life's inevitable transitions. These skills help you manage the changes that come your way and empower you to seek out and create positive outcomes. Remember these strategies the next time you face a shift and confidently move forward.

BUILDING RESILIENCE: BOUNCING BACK FROM SETBACKS

Resilience is like a superpower you can develop. It's the ability to bounce back from tough times and recover from difficulties. Imagine a rubber band that stretches but doesn't break—that's what resilience feels like. It's crucial for personal development because life isn't always smooth sailing. Sometimes, it throws curveballs that test your patience and strength. But resilience isn't just about enduring hardships; it's about learning from them and growing stronger. Endurance is about surviving the storm, while resilience is about thriving in spite of it. The more resilient you become, the more prepared you are to tackle future challenges confidently and gracefully.

Learning from setbacks is an integral part of building resilience. What might feel like a defeat is actually a stepping stone to success. Many famous individuals faced challenges before achieving greatness. Take Thomas Edison, for instance. He failed many times before the light bulb became a reality. Instead of giving up, he treated each mistake as a lesson on what didn't work. This mindset helped him refine his approach until he found success. When things don't go as planned, try to see the experience as valuable feedback. Ask yourself, "What can be learned from this?" Evaluate what went wrong and how you can improve next time. This approach turns failures into powerful learning opportunities that build resilience (Life Coach Training, n.d.).

Cultivating a positive outlook is like planting seeds of optimism that grow even in challenging times. Although mentioned in a previous chapter, affirmations and visualization are especially relevant to the topic of maintaining positivity. Affirmations are uplifting statements that remind you of your strengths and highlight your potential. Say them aloud or write them down, like, "I have the strength to overcome challenges and achieve my goals." Visualization involves imagining yourself succeeding in a situation. Picture the details, like how you'll feel and what you'll do. This mental rehearsal boosts confidence and prepares you for real-life challenges. By combining affirmations and visualization, you create a positive mindset that helps you face challenges with confidence.

Building problem-solving skills is important for resilience because life loves throwing unexpected challenges your way. A good place to start is by practicing critical thinking with "what if" scenarios. Here's an example. What if your best friend suddenly stopped talking to you, and you weren't sure why? How would you handle the situation—would you reach out, give them space, or ask a mutual friend for insight? Imagine different situations and think on your feet to find possible solutions. You can also brainstorm with friends or classmates. Tackling hypothetical challenges as a group is fun, and everyone's unique perspective adds fresh ideas. Plus, it's a great way to boost your teamwork and problem-solving skills. It's like assembling a team of superheroes, each with their own powers, ready to tackle any obstacle (Life Coach Training, n.d.).

Resilience isn't about having a stress-free life but developing the skills to handle stress and setbacks effectively. By embracing failures as learning opportunities, maintaining a positive outlook, and honing problem-solving skills, you equip yourself with the means to navigate life's challenges. These strategies build a strong foundation of resilience, enabling you to face hardship with courage and determination. So, when life gets tough, remember that resilience gives you the strength to adapt, learn, and keep moving forward.

NEW BEGINNINGS: ADJUSTING TO NEW ENVIRONMENTS

Adjusting to a new environment can feel like stepping into an unfamiliar world. Everything seems different, from the people to the way things work. It's natural to feel a mix of excitement and anxiety about what's ahead. Preparing mentally and emotionally can make this transition smoother. Start by doing a little research about your new surroundings using your favorite search engine or

AI assistant. Whether it's a new school or a different community, learning about the culture, norms, and routines can help you feel more comfortable about the unknowns. This preparation is like studying a map before a trip; it gives you a sense of direction and familiarity. Set realistic expectations for the change. Remember that adjusting might take time, but that's perfectly okay. Expect a few bumps along the way, and remind yourself that you're capable of navigating through them.

Meeting new people, in addition to being in an unfamiliar place, can be both exciting and nerve-wracking. It's like stepping into a room full of strangers and wondering who might turn out to be your next friend. To help ease you into this, start with simple ice-breaker activities. These are a casual way to get to know others, help break the initial awkwardness, and even pave the way for deeper connections. A helpful skill when entering a new space is to be observant. Take a moment to examine your surroundings and look for clues about shared interests. For instance, does someone have a backpack with a patch from your favorite game or TV show? Maybe you spot a logo for a sports team you like or notice someone wearing a style similar to yours, like a fabulous pair of shoes. These observations can serve as natural conversation starters, helping you know what to say after your name. So smile, step forward, and introduce yourself. When it comes to encouraging dialogue, a good tip is to ask open-ended questions. Instead of, "Did you have a good weekend?" try, "What did you do over the weekend?" Phrasing them this way invites the other person to share more about themselves, making it easier to find common ground and keep the conversation flowing. Listening actively and showing genuine interest in what others have to say can also make you more approachable and likable.

While you're busy making new friends, it's important not to lose touch with the old ones. These are the people who know you best and can offer support during this transition. Scheduling regular catch-ups through video calls, texting, or emailing can help maintain those connections. Use technology to your advantage. Create group chats, stream watch parties, or enjoy online games together —whatever keeps you connected. Balancing old and new relationships is like weaving a tapestry. The threads of your past relationships provide strength and stability, while new connections add vibrant colors and patterns to your life.

Sometimes, the unknown can feel intimidating, like standing at the edge of a dark forest. But it can also be exciting if you let it be. Instead of fearing what's unfamiliar, view it as a blank canvas full of possibilities. Embrace the uncertainty as a chance to discover new opportunities and foster personal growth. Open your journaling app and write about your hopes and fears, what excites you about the change, and any concerns you may have. Reflecting on these thoughts helps clarify your feelings and prepares you emotionally. Over time, you may find that the things you once feared have become sources of joy and strength.

New beginnings are a part of life, filled with challenges and opportunities. With preparation and an open mind, you can navigate these transitions confidently. Whether you're meeting new people or embracing the unknown, each step forward builds resilience and adaptability. So go ahead and explore your next chapter with curiosity and courage.

THE POWER OF FLEXIBILITY: ADAPTING PLANS AND GOALS

Imagine you're on a road trip with a well-planned route, but halfway through, you hit a detour sign. Flexibility in planning is like having a map that shows alternate paths when your original route is blocked. It's essential because life rarely goes as planned, and being able to adjust can make all the difference. Consider a flexible goal-setting technique like the SMART method discussed in Chapter 4. Using this approach helps you set clear goals and allows room for change. If something isn't working, you can tweak the "Achievable" part without losing sight of your end goal. Consider visionaries like Elon Musk, who often pivot in response to new information or challenges. Their ability to adapt plans has led to groundbreaking innovations. Flexibility doesn't mean abandoning your goals. It's about finding new ways to reach them when things don't go as expected.

Balancing structure and flexibility is like walking a tightrope. You need a plan but must also be ready to sway with the wind. To maintain this balance, start by creating adaptable action plans. These plans have built-in flexibility, like contingency options or backup strategies. For instance, if you're planning a picnic with friends, have a plan B for bad weather. To revise your plans, try setting regular check-ins to see how things are going and make any necessary changes. This way, you're not rigidly sticking to a plan that's no longer relevant. It's like cooking with a recipe—you follow the instructions while tasting and adjusting to your liking. This adaptability ensures you stay on track while remaining open to better options.

The concept of pivoting is crucial when initial plans don't pan out. It's the skill of changing direction while keeping your goals in sight. Successful businesses often pivot to adapt to new markets or technologies. Take Netflix, for example. They started as a DVD rental service and pivoted to streaming as digital technology advanced. This shift saved the company and made it a leader in the industry. Think of Uber and Lyft. They'll need to pivot with the rollout of driverless taxis. When faced with a setback, assess the situation, gather information, and identify new opportunities. Think of it as changing the sails to catch a new wind rather than abandoning the ship. Pivoting requires a blend of creativity and practicality, allowing you to find success even when your original plan doesn't work.

A weekly review of any progress or setbacks is helpful for staying adaptable. It's about regularly checking in on your goals to see where you stand and where adjustments are needed. This structured reflection helps you identify patterns and make informed decisions about changes. Include reflective questions for self-assessment, such as, "What have I learned so far?" or "What can I do differently?" These questions encourage introspection and growth.

Evaluating progress isn't just about tracking success—it's about learning from setbacks and using those lessons to move forward more effectively. With these strategies, flexibility becomes a powerful ally in achieving your goals, transforming obstacles into milestones on the path to success.

FINDING YOUR JOY: EXPLORING NEW PASSIONS AND INTERESTS

Have you ever wondered what truly excites you? Discovering your passions and interests is like finding hidden gems within yourself. It's a journey of self-exploration that can guide you toward a fulfilling path in life. To get started, try some self-discovery activities. One effective method is taking an interest and skill inventory, which involves listing things you enjoy doing and identifying the skills you naturally excel in. Maybe you're athletic and enjoy team activities, love painting with watercolors, or have a knack for solving puzzles. Write these down and reflect on how they make you feel. This exercise helps you see patterns in your interests and reveals areas worth exploring further.

Once you've identified potential interests, it's time to dive deeper by exploring hobbies through clubs or workshops. Joining a club at school or your place of worship or participating in a local workshop can expose you to new experiences and connect you with like-minded individuals. Whether it's a photography club, camp counselor internship, or a coding workshop, these activities allow you to test the waters and see if your interest grows into a passion. They also provide a mentor-rich environment where you can learn and grow alongside others who share similar interests. This exploration can lead to exciting discoveries about yourself and open up new avenues for personal growth.

Aligning your interests with your life goals is like connecting the dots on a map, guiding you toward a destination that brings satisfaction and motivation. To visualize this alignment, try creating a vision board. Gather images, quotes, and symbols representing your aspirations and the things you love. Organize them in a space, physical or digital, where you can view them frequently. This visual tool is a daily reminder of what you're working towards and keeps you focused on your goals. Additionally, set short-term goals related to your interests. If you love music, a short-term goal might be learning to read sheet music. These goals keep you motivated and moving forward.

Keep an open mind when exploring your passions. Sometimes, what you think you'll love might not be what you expected, while unexpected interests can spark new passions. Try diverse extracurricular activities, even if they seem outside your comfort zone. For example, there are several sports to check out. Volunteering in different fields is another excellent way to gain exposure to new experiences. You might discover a passion for community service programs that assist older adults, learn about animals through 4-H, or explore environmental conservation to help the planet. These opportunities allow you to learn about different aspects of life and develop a broader perspective. Embrace the unknown and be open to the surprises it can bring.

Building a personal pathway is about crafting a flexible plan for pursuing your interests and potential career paths. Start by mapping out a personalized roadmap with clear milestones that align with your goals. Identify the steps needed to reach your goals and break them into smaller, achievable tasks. For example, suppose you aspire to be a writer. In that case, your roadmap might include milestones like joining a local writing club, participating in online writing workshops, interviewing a published author, and contributing to your school newspaper or yearbook. This roadmap is your guide, helping you stay on track while allowing room for adjustments as you grow and learn. It's a dynamic process that evolves with you, ensuring you remain aligned with your passions and aspirations.

Finding your path is a continuous process of exploration, alignment, open-mindedness, and planning. Each step brings you closer to understanding who you are and what you want to achieve. As you explore your interests and build your personal pathway, you're not just discovering passions but creating a life that reflects your unique self. Keep an open heart and mind as you navigate this exciting phase of self-discovery, recognizing that each experience contributes to the rich and unique story of who you are.

CHAPTER 9
DISCOVERING PURPOSE AND DIRECTION

"Efforts and courage are not enough without purpose and direction."

JOHN F. KENNEDY

You may not want to be president, but have you ever found yourself lost in thought, dreaming about turning your passion for doodling into a comic book series or your love for coding into the next viral app? That's the magic of passion projects. They're like taking a piece of your imagination and bringing it to life. Passion projects let you dive deep into what you love and create something unique. Whether art, spirituality, technology, animals, or social causes, passion projects offer a space to explore your interests, gain new skills, and grow as a person.

PASSION PROJECTS: TURNING INTERESTS INTO OPPORTUNITIES

Finding out what truly excites you is the first step in creating a passion project. Use the details from Chapter 8, the section on Finding Your Joy, or the Interactive Element prompt below. Once you have this information, it's time to transform your interests into a passion project. Think of a project as a journey with a destination—clear objectives and steps to get there. Start by setting specific goals for what you want to achieve. If you're passionate about photography, perhaps your project is to create a photo exhibition showcasing the beauty and symmetry in architecture. Outline the steps needed to reach your goal, from selecting themes and taking photographs to editing and organizing the exhibit. Consider what resources you'll need, like a camera, transportation to the buildings, editing software, or even mentors to guide you. Breaking it down into manageable parts makes the project less daunting and more achievable. It's like assembling a puzzle one piece at a time, each step bringing you closer to the complete picture (Yang, 2023).

Passion projects are more than just fulfilling; they're catalysts for growth. Document your progress and any challenges you overcome in a journal or digital log. Note what you tried, what worked, and what didn't, so you can reflect on this and continue improving. Your documentation serves a purpose—it's a reflection of your learning, insights, and growth. This process helps you learn from mistakes and reminds you to celebrate successes. These projects introduce you to potential friends and open doors to new opportunities, such as scholarships or internships, by demonstrating your initiative and dedication.

Interactive Element: *Creating Your Interest Inventory*

Take a moment to create your own interest inventory. Write down activities that excite you, and next to each one, note why they matter to you. Reflect on these interests and consider how they could evolve into a passion project. This exercise will help you uncover potential projects and their value to your personal growth.

When it comes to showcasing your passion project, think of it in terms of your personal brand. Create a portfolio that highlights your work, whether digital or physical. Depending on your project, it could be a website, a video presentation, a display board, or a scrapbook. A well-organized portfolio shows off your hard work and tells a story of your passion and creativity. Imagine presenting your project at a school event or as part of a college application. The key is to communicate your enthusiasm and your project's impact on you and others. Preparing a speech or presentation about your project can further enhance your communication skills and confidence. Practice with friends or family to refine your delivery and ensure your passion shines through (Yang, 2023).

By turning your passions into projects, you're not just pursuing what you love but building a foundation for future success. Passion projects are about discovering what makes you tick and using that knowledge to create something meaningful and impactful. They're an opportunity to learn, grow, and express yourself in ways traditional learning might not offer. As you embark on your passion project, remember that the experiences you gain along the way hold as much value as the final outcome.

CAREER EXPLORATION: FINDING YOUR FIT IN THE WORLD OF WORK

Thinking about your future career might feel like looking at a massive menu and not knowing what to order. There are so many options, and each one seems to come with its own set of skills and challenges. But fear not, because researching career options can help determine what suits you best. Start by using online career assessment tools; these are like quizzes that match your interests and skills with potential career paths. They're fun and enlightening, offering a glimpse into jobs you might not have previously considered. Websites like onetonline.org (O*NET Online) and youth.gov are treasure troves of information, offering detailed descriptions of various occupations, including the skills needed, the work environment, and the expected salary. Diving into these resources helps you understand what different careers entail and how they align with your interests.

Once you have a few career options in mind, gaining hands-on experience becomes invaluable. Internships, job shadowing, and volunteer work are fantastic ways to test the waters. They allow you to step into a professional setting and see what a day in the life of a particular job looks like. Your school may already have some options lined up, so check with the career counselor. In addition, look around your local community for opportunities in fields that interest you. Libraries, animal shelters, hospitals, tech companies, or even local businesses might offer internships or shadowing opportunities. Don't hesitate to reach out to professionals for informational interviews. These are informal chats where you can ask questions about their career path, the industry, and any advice they might have for someone just starting out. It's like getting insider tips from someone who has walked the path you're considering (Youth.gov, n.d.).

Understanding the job market is like having a map when you're entering unknown territory. Staying informed about current job market trends can guide your career decisions. Research which skills and industries are in high demand. O*NET Online is great for this. This knowledge helps you tailor your education and skill development to meet market needs. Analyzing job market reports can also reveal future trends, showing which industries are growing and which might be fading. This foresight helps you make informed decisions about which career paths to pursue, equipping yourself with the skills employers are seeking. By staying updated on these trends, you're not just planning for the present but preparing for the future.

Building a professional network is a crucial step in your career exploration. There's a popular saying: "It's not what you know, it's who you know." It's about connecting with people who can offer guidance, support, and opportunities. Start by attending career fairs, workshops, and seminars related to your areas of interest. These events are excellent places to meet industry professionals and learn about different careers. Remember to follow up with the contacts you make—send a thank-you email or connect with them on LinkedIn. Speaking of LinkedIn, creating a profile there is a smart move. It's like your digital resume, showcasing your skills, experiences, and interests to potential employers and mentors. Join professional groups related to your career interests, where you can participate in discussions and gain insights from experienced individuals. Networking is not just about finding a job; it's about building relationships that can support your career growth over time (Ennis-O'Connor, 2023).

Networking might seem daunting at first, but think of it as making new friends who share your interests. When you approach it with curiosity and an open mind, it becomes less about selling yourself and more about learning from others. Practice effective networking strategies both in-person and online. Be genuine in your interactions, dress appropriately, listen more than you speak, and always look for ways to offer value to others. Whether sharing a helpful article or connecting two people who might benefit from knowing each other, these small gestures build goodwill and strengthen your network. Through these connections, you not only learn about different career paths but also gain mentors who can guide you as you navigate your professional life.

SETTING YOUR COURSE: CRAFTING A PERSONAL VISION STATEMENT

A personal vision statement is like a compass, guiding you through life's twists and turns and aligning you with who you truly are. It's a clear and concise declaration of your values, dreams, and the impact you want to make. How is this different from our original mission statement? A vision statement focuses on where you want to go, while your mission statement highlights what you're doing now to get there. Crafting one might seem daunting, but it starts with understanding what honestly matters to you. Consider examples from leaders or mentors you admire. Their vision statements might speak about innovation, compassion, or empowerment. Yours should reflect your unique aspirations and ideals. Begin with a simple writing exercise: jot down what you love doing, what you're good at, and what you believe the world needs. These notes form the foundation of your vision statement, capturing your essence in words. This process encourages self-reflection, helping you recognize what drives you and how you want to contribute to the world (Imbastoni, 2023).

Once you have a draft, the next step is aligning it with your core values and long-term goals. Reflect on your principles and what you stand for. Maybe you value honesty, creativity, or community service. These values should resonate throughout your vision statement, like a steady beat in a song. Consider where you see yourself in the future. Your vision statement should reflect your current passions and guide you toward your long-term dreams. It's your compass, keeping you on course even when life gets hectic. By ensuring your vision aligns with your values and goals, you create an original and motivating statement. This alignment helps you stay true to yourself, especially when faced with tough decisions or new opportunities.

Refining your vision statement is like sculpting a piece of clay. It requires time, patience, and a willingness to shape and reshape until it reflects your authentic vision. Share your draft with trusted friends or mentors and invite their constructive feedback. These peer review sessions offer fresh perspectives, helping you see angles you might have missed. It's like getting a second pair of eyes on your work, ensuring it reflects your true intentions. Listen to their insights, but remember that the final statement should still feel personal to you. As you refine it, aim for clear and concise wording. A strong vision statement is specific enough to guide you yet broad enough to grow with you over time. It should inspire you every time you read it, reminding you what you're striving for and why (Imbastoni, 2023).

Your vision statement becomes a powerful tool when you use it as a decision-making guide. Whenever you're unsure about a choice, revisit it and ask yourself if the decision aligns with your vision statement. This practice helps prioritize opportunities that resonate with your goals and values, making decisions less over-whelming. Think of it as your personal North Star. Over time, revisit and revise your vision statement. Your experiences and perspectives might shift as you grow, and that's okay. Your statement should evolve alongside you, reflecting new insights and aspirations. By consistently aligning your actions with your vision, you build a meaningful and fulfilling life.

THE ROAD AHEAD: PLANNING FOR THE FUTURE WITH CONFIDENCE

Planning for the future might feel like planting a garden—you start with a patch of soil and a vision. Setting long-term goals is like planting seeds, nurturing them over time to grow into the life you've imagined. Start by considering your life aspirations and how they align with your vision. Break these big dreams into smaller, actionable steps that you can tackle individually. Imagine wanting to become a graphic designer. Begin by learning basic design tools, take a few online courses, and then offer your services to a local non-profit for their next fundraiser to gain real-world experience. Each step builds on the last, bringing you closer to your ultimate goal. This method makes big goals feel more achievable and keeps you motivated, as you can see the progress you're making.

Creating a strategic action plan is a way to map out your journey, with timelines and milestones marking your path. Think of it as setting up checkpoints that keep you on track. Start by listing the steps you need to take for each goal, then assign a timeline. Suppose your goal is to learn to play the guitar. In that case, your plan might include finding a teacher within two weeks, daily practice sessions, building a repertoire of a few songs you enjoy, and performing at an open mic night within eight months. Having these milestones helps you measure your progress and adjust your plans as needed. Use a planner or app to organize these tasks, making it easier to stay on schedule. Sample strategic plan templates are available online, offering a structured outline of your goals and actions. This planning stage transforms your aspirations into tangible steps, providing order and purpose.

But let's be real—life doesn't always go according to plan. Obstacles will come your way, and staying motivated can be tough. The key is learning to navigate setbacks without losing sight of your goals. When things don't go as expected, take a moment to reassess the situation. What went wrong, and how can you overcome it? This reflection turns obstacles into learning opportunities, helping you grow stronger and more resilient. Maintain your focus by surrounding yourself with reminders of your goals. Create a playlist filled with motivational songs that ignite and energize you. Or craft a vision board filled with images and quotes that resonate with your aspirations. These visual and auditory cues can spark your passion and move you forward, even if the path is rocky.

Reviewing and adjusting your plans is crucial to ensuring they remain relevant and achievable. Set up regular meetings with a mentor or a trusted friend to discuss your progress and any obstacles you've encountered. These sessions allow you to gain new perspectives and advice on your journey. Use this time to celebrate your achievements, no matter how small, and reassess your goals as needed. Life is dynamic, and your plans should be too. As you learn and grow, it's okay if your aspirations shift. Adjusting your plans ensures they continue to align with your evolving values and goals. It's like tuning your guitar; regular adjustments keep you in harmony with your vision and ready to face whatever comes next.

SUCCESS STORIES: LEARNING FROM REAL-LIFE ROLE MODELS

Have you ever looked at someone and thought, "Wow, I want to be like them!"? That's the power of a role model. These individuals shine in their fields and offer a roadmap to success. The first step in tapping into this power is finding role models who resonate with your interests. Dive into biographies and stories of people who've achieved greatness in areas you're passionate about. Whether it's a groundbreaking scientist, a devout spiritual leader, a talented artist, or a compassionate activist, their stories offer a wealth of inspiration. As you read, pay attention to their common traits and habits. You might notice that many successful people have a strong work ethic, resilience, and a knack for innovation. Understanding these traits can give you clues about what it takes to succeed in your chosen field (Fox, 2023).

Learning from the journeys of role models is like peeking behind the curtain of their success. Each victory is often the result of overcoming numerous challenges. Look for case studies or interviews that detail their paths, highlighting both the highs and the lows. These stories are packed with valuable lessons and insights. Take someone like Oprah Winfrey, who overcame significant obstacles before becoming a media powerhouse and philanthropist. Her story teaches resilience, self-belief, and the power of pursuing your passions. As you explore these journeys, consider questions that dig deeper: What obstacles did they overcome? How did they stay motivated? What specific steps did they take to reach their goals? These questions help you analyze their experiences and extract lessons you can use in your own life.

The real magic happens when you apply these lessons to your personal goals. Reflective writing exercises can be a great way to do this. Grab a notebook or open a Word document and jot down the key takeaways from your role model's journey. How can their strategies and mindset help you achieve your dreams? Maybe it's their dedication to daily practice or their ability to pivot when faced with failure. Reflect on how these lessons resonate with your current situation. This exercise isn't just about copying their path;

it's about adapting their wisdom to fit your unique journey. By doing so, you can pursue your passions with the same tenacity.

Connecting with role models might feel intimidating, but it's more accessible than you think. Start by crafting a professional outreach email or letter. Introduce yourself, express admiration for their work, and mention specific ways their journey has inspired you. Be genuine and concise, and don't forget to thank them for their time. You'd be surprised how many people are willing to share advice and guidance, especially when approached with respect and sincerity. Another suggestion is to follow them on social media and comment on their posts to build a rapport. Consider attending events where your role models might speak or participate, like conferences, book signings, or online webinars. These gatherings provide opportunities to hear directly from those you admire and, if you're lucky, to engage in conversation. Remember, the goal isn't just to meet them but to learn and grow from their insights.

Role models provide valuable examples of navigating challenges and working toward success. By identifying, learning from, and connecting with these inspiring individuals, you gain wisdom and the motivation to pursue your dreams with renewed energy. Their stories show us that success is built on learning from others, drawing inspiration from their ability to overcome adversity, and applying those lessons to our own journeys.

CHAPTER 10

CULTIVATING A BALANCED LIFESTYLE

"Almost everything will work again if you unplug it for a few minutes, including you."

ANNE LAMOTT

This quote might make you smile, but it also taps into an essential truth about the need to find balance and reconnect with yourself. Imagine your life as a juggling act—keeping everything in the air takes focus, timing, and knowing when to let something rest for a moment. Creating a healthy lifestyle is a lot like that. It's about finding your rhythm and making minor, consistent adjustments to maintain your well-being. From establishing a daily routine to embracing healthier eating and incorporating regular exercise, building a balanced lifestyle can transform how you feel and function every day.

HEALTHY HABITS: BUILDING A ROUTINE FOR WELLNESS

Each day offers a fresh start, a blank slate to write on with purpose and intention. Establishing a daily routine can be your secret weapon in creating a balanced and fulfilling life. Start with morning rituals that set a positive tone for the day. Even little things have an impact, like making your bed and reading an affirmation. Consider earmarking time for stretching, prayer, or meditation. Stretching engages your muscles and improves circulation, preparing you for what lies ahead. Prayer and meditation are like quiet oases for your mind, helping you find peace before beginning the day. Whether it's five minutes or fifteen, this time is sacred. It enables you to center yourself, reducing stress and enhancing focus.

A consistent sleep schedule is another cornerstone of wellness. Like charging your phone overnight, sleep restores your energy and prepares you for the next day. Seven to nine hours of sleep are recommended to fully recharge your body and mind. Maintain a consistent sleep schedule by going to bed and waking up at the same time each day, including weekends. This consistency will assist in regulating your internal clock and improve your sleep quality. It's tempting to stay up late scrolling through social media or binge-watching shows, but you'll feel much better throughout the day if you choose to rest instead. Your tomorrow self will thank you.

Physical activity is like fuel for your body, keeping it strong and healthy. Regular exercise builds strong bones, boosts muscle strength, and even improves your mood by releasing endorphins—those feel-good chemicals that make you happy. Incorporating physical activity into your day doesn't have to complicate it. Consider simple exercises like walking, yoga, or even playing a team sport. Walking is a fantastic, low-impact activity that you can do almost anywhere, and the family dog will love it, too. Yoga strengthens your body and calms your mind, offering flexibility and peace. If you enjoy competition and camaraderie, joining a sports team can be a fun way to stay active while making friends. Create a weekly workout plan that includes a mix of these activities. This plan can guide you in staying active and ensuring you get a variety of exercises throughout the week (Kaiser Permanente, 2023).

Eating well is a vital part of maintaining a balanced lifestyle. It's about fueling your body with the proper nutrients to keep it running smoothly. Start by planning balanced meals that feature a variety of fruits, vegetables, and proteins. Fruits and vegetables are packed with vitamins and minerals, while proteins help build and repair tissues. Meal preparation apps and cookbooks will ensure balanced meals that keep you energized and satisfied. Speaking of cookbooks, this is a good time to segue into learning how to cook. Being in control of meal preparation and understanding nutrition labels empowers you to make healthier food choices. Check for serving sizes and calorie data to understand the necessity of portion control, and review nutritional information to ensure you're eating well-rounded meals. Embrace cooking as a way to build healthy habits and take you another step closer to independence.

Interactive Element: *Weekly Wellness Planner*

Create a wellness planner to track your daily routines, physical activities, and meals. Divide your planner into sections for each aspect of wellness: morning rituals, exercise, and nutrition. Use this planner to set intentions for the week, noting activities and meals you plan to incorporate. Reflect on your progress at the end of each week, celebrating successes and identifying areas for improvement. This visual tool can help you maintain focus and consistency on your journey to a balanced lifestyle.

Taking small, intentional steps toward creating a balanced lifestyle can profoundly impact your overall well-being. Establishing a daily routine, incorporating physical activity, getting consistent sleep, and being mindful of your nutrition, build a foundation for a healthier, happier life. Each day is an opportunity to make choices that support your well-being. With time and practice, these healthy habits will become second nature. So take a deep breath, embrace the journey, and remember that wellness is within your reach.

BALANCING ACT: HARMONIZING HOBBIES AND RESPONSIBILITIES

Finding the right balance between your responsibilities and hobbies can feel like walking a fine line between staying productive and making time for yourself. Getting caught up in schoolwork, chores, and other commitments is easy, leaving little room for the things you love. However, identifying core responsibilities is key to managing your time effectively. Start by creating a priority list that highlights what needs your attention first. Schoolwork might take a top spot because, let's face it, assignments and exams have deadlines that won't wait. Chores might follow, especially if you're part of a household team. Once you've mapped out these essentials, you'll have a clearer picture of how much time you have remaining for everything else. This list helps you stay organized and prevents those last-minute panics when tasks pile up (Harvard University, 2022).

Now, let's talk about making room for your hobbies—the things that light you up and give you joy. Integrating them into your daily life doesn't mean neglecting your responsibilities. Instead, it's about thoughtful planning. Consider what was recommended in Chapter 4: using time-blocking techniques to carve out specific periods for your hobbies. To reiterate, think of your day as a series of blocks dedicated to a different task or activity. Allocating a particular time for your hobby ensures it doesn't get sidelined. For example, if you love painting, set aside a block each afternoon to dive into your art. This method helps you stay disciplined, as you know exactly when you'll get to enjoy your hobby, and it keeps you from feeling guilty about taking time away from other tasks.

Creative scheduling can also be your ally in finding harmony between work and play. Explore different ways to fit your hobbies into your life without feeling overwhelmed. For example, try combining them with other activities. If you're into music, listen to your favorite tunes while doing chores or during your commute. If reading is your thing, bring a book to enjoy during lunch breaks or while waiting for the bus. The key is to make your hobbies a seamless part of your routine so they don't feel like an extra task. This creative approach means you're not just squeezing hobbies into your schedule; you're weaving them into the fabric of your day.

Downtime is another crucial aspect of maintaining balance. It's the unscheduled, unstructured time that lets you recharge and reset. Don't underestimate the power of doing nothing. Downtime fosters creativity and relaxation, allowing your mind to wander and explore new ideas. Allow yourself moments for spontaneous activities, like walking, doodling, or simply daydreaming. These breaks are not wasted time; they're vital for your mental health and well-being.

Setting realistic expectations is essential to balancing hobbies and responsibilities without feeling stretched too thin. It's easy to get excited and overcommit, thinking you can do it all. But remember, you're human, not a superhero. Teach yourself to set achievable goals that align with your priorities. Develop a weekly balance checklist that outlines what you hope to accomplish in both areas. This checklist keeps you accountable and helps you track your progress. At the end of each week, take a moment to reflect. What went well? Where did you struggle? Use these insights to make adjustments and improvements for the following week. This process of reflection and adjustment ensures you're not just busy but productive and fulfilled (Harvard University, 2022).

Balancing your responsibilities and hobbies is an ongoing process that requires patience and flexibility. It's about finding what works for you and being kind to yourself when things don't go as planned. By identifying your core responsibilities, creatively integrating your hobbies, valuing downtime, and setting realistic expectations, you're laying the groundwork for a balanced and fulfilling life. Remember, it's not about perfection; it's about progress and creating a lifestyle that supports your passions and commitments.

LIVING AUTHENTICALLY: STAYING TRUE TO YOURSELF IN EVERY SITUATION

Living authentically is all about understanding who you are at your core. It sounds simple, yet many people spend a lifetime figuring it out. It starts with identifying your personal values. These are the principles and beliefs that guide your choices and actions. They define who you are and what you stand for. Take some time to reflect on what matters most to you. Is it honesty, kindness, creativity, or perhaps a sense of adventure? Write these values down and think about how they influence your daily life.

To dive deeper into identifying your core values, try a writing exercise where you explore your reactions to different situations. It can reveal patterns and help pinpoint them. For instance, recall a time when you felt proud of yourself or stood up for something you believed in. Maybe you stood up to a friend who was being unkind to someone at school, driven by your sense of fairness or compassion. Identifying the underlying value in such moments helps create a values-based decision-making framework. This framework acts like a compass, guiding you through life's many choices with confidence and clarity.

Expressing your individuality is about showing the world who you are without holding back. It's embracing those quirks and unique qualities that make you, you. Developing a personal style is one way to do this. It could be through fashion, music, or even the way you speak. Your style reflects your personality, and it's okay to experiment until you find what feels right. It might be those funky socks that make you smile or that playlist that perfectly captures your vibe. Whatever it is, own it with pride.

Sharing your passions with peers is another way to express yourself confidently. Whether it's a hidden talent for drawing or a budding interest in fashion, letting others see your passions can be empowering and inspiring. Start by talking to friends about your interests or joining a club where you can share your skills. Not only does this build confidence, but it also connects you with people who appreciate your uniqueness.

Maintaining integrity can be challenging, especially in tough situations. It's about staying true to your values even when it's difficult, like when you face peer pressure. Imagine being in a scenario where you're pressured to do something that doesn't align with your beliefs. Role-playing these situations can prepare you for real-life dilemmas. Gather a group of friends and create scenarios where ethical decision-making is required. Practice standing firm in your values while respecting others' perspectives. This exercise strengthens your resolve and helps you act with integrity when faced with real challenges.

Building a supportive environment is crucial for living authentically. Surround yourself with people who encourage and celebrate your true self. They are your support network. Positive relationships are like sunlight, helping you grow and flourish. Identify those friends and mentors who lift you up and make you feel valued. Spend time with them, and don't be afraid to distance yourself from toxic or constricting influences. It's okay to prioritize your well-being and choose relationships that nurture your authenticity.

Living authentically is an ongoing process, and it takes courage and self-awareness. It's about embracing your true self, expressing it boldly, and navigating life with integrity. By understanding your values, expressing your individuality, maintaining integrity, and building a strong support network, you're well on your way to living a life that's true to who you are. Your authenticity is your superpower, with the potential to positively impact your life and the lives of those around you by being an ally to others. As you continue to explore and grow, remember that staying true to yourself is one of the most empowering things you can do.

CONCLUSION

Wow, what a journey we've been on together! From the first page to this conclusion, you've explored a treasure trove of life skills that are key to navigating the path to adulthood. Whether you're gearing up for your first job, seeking new passions, learning to manage your time, or figuring out how to navigate the digital world responsibly, you've gathered tools that will serve you well beyond these pages.

Let's take a moment to reflect on what's been covered. We've focused on boosting self-confidence because, let's face it, having faith in your own potential is the first step to tackling anything. We've explored financial literacy, showing you how to budget and save so your wallet isn't empty when you need it most. Communication skills came next; we discussed speaking up and listening actively, which are crucial in any relationship. Time management tips helped you find balance in a busy world, while stress management techniques taught you how to find calm in chaos. Navigating relationships gave you the tools to set boundaries and build trust. Our digital citizenship section showed you how to be savvy and safe online. Adaptability and resilience equipped you to bounce back from setbacks, while the chapters on discovering purpose and cultivating a balanced lifestyle guided you in aligning your daily actions with your dreams and values.

In each chapter, you've encountered practical strategies and exercises designed to turn theory into action. From mindful breathing to wellness planning, budgeting to banking, role-playing to journaling, these different activities were crafted to help you practice and internalize what you've learned. The goal was to empower you, giving you the confidence to apply these skills in real-life situations. Reflect on your journey. How have the lessons influenced your conviction and outlook? Think about the changes you've made and the new ones you still want to pursue. Dream big, and confidently take the next step.

As you near the end of this book, take a moment to acknowledge how far you've come. You've grown, adapted, and built a toolkit of skills that will help you face life's challenges head-on. Each step you've taken is a victory in its own right, so celebrate your achievements. But the adventure isn't over—it continues every day. Keep practicing these skills by joining clubs, seeking mentors, or volunteering in your community. Opportunities for continued learning are everywhere.

Before we part, I want to express my gratitude for allowing me to be part of your journey. Thank you for embracing this path with an open heart and mind. Your commitment to personal development is commendable, so I urge you to share your story and inspire others.

Remember, you are empowered! You're capable, strong, and ready to face whatever the future holds. You've got the life skills to navigate young adulthood with confidence and grace. Keep believing in yourself, keep learning, and keep growing. The world is full of possibilities, and with your skills and determination, you're ready to make it amazing.

HELP OTHERS START THEIR JOURNEY

Now that you've explored all the tools and tips to boost your confidence and sharpen your life skills, it's time to share your experience with others.

By leaving an honest review of *Empowered! Life Skills for Teens* on Amazon, you're helping other teens and parents discover a resource that can guide them through the same exciting journey. Your insights might be exactly what someone needs to take their first step toward growth and success.

Thank you for helping empower more teens with these life skills. Your feedback makes a difference and helps me continue to inspire and support others.

- Casey

REFERENCES

Ackerman, C. E. (2019, February 4). *13 emotional intelligence exercises, activities &* *worksheets*. Positive Psychology. https://positivepsychology.com/emotional-intelligence-exercises/

Asana. (2024, January 29). *The Eisenhower Matrix: How to prioritize your to-do list*. https://asana.com/resources/eisenhower-matrix

Barrell, A. (2020, June 2). *5 breathing exercises for anxiety and how to do them*. Medical News Today. https://www.medicalnewstoday.com/articles/breathing-exercises-for-anxiety

Batchelor, M. (2021, August 31). *How your digital footprint can impact your career*. The CEO Magazine. https://www.theceomagazine.com/business/hr/digital-footprint-impacts-career/

Chang, J. (2023, March 24). *Compound interest 101: The benefits of saving early*. Northwestern Mutual. https://www.northwesternmutual.com/life-and-money/compound-interest-101-the-benefits-of-saving-early/

Cleveland Clinic. (2021, November 23). *How to do a digital detox for less stress, more focus*. Cleveland Clinic Health Essentials. https://health.clevelandclinic.org/digital-detox

Covey, S. R. (1989). *The 7 habits of highly effective people: Powerful lessons in personal change*. Free Press.

Cullins, A. (n.d.). *9 self-confidence building activities for students*. Big Life Journal. https://biglifejournal.com/blogs/blog/self-confidence-building-activities?

Ennis-O'Connor, M. (2023, July 1). *How to build a professional network on LinkedIn*. LinkedIn. https://www.linkedin.com/pulse/how-build-professional-network-linkedin-marie-ennis-o-connor/

Foster, S. J. (2024, August 29). *Creating a calming space: Relaxation techniques for teens at home*. Medium. https://medium.com/@sarahjuliafoster/creating-a-calming-space-relaxation-techniques-for-teens-at-home-433df38d2e27

Fox, M. (2023, November 5). *Teen titans: 13 young people making an outsized positive impact*. Forbes. https://www.forbes.com/sites/meimeifox/2023/11/05/teen-titans-13-young-people-making-an-outsized-positive-impact/

Go Moment. (n.d.). *How to practice active listening in conversations*. https://go-moment.com/how-to-practice-active-listening-in-conversations/

Gomez, S. (n.d.). *If you have three people in your life that you can trust, you can consider yourself the luckiest person in the whole world* [Quote]. The Wordy Boy. https://thewordyboy.com/trust-quotes-by-world-famous-personalities/

Hamid, M. (n.d.). *Empathy is about finding echoes of another person in yourself* [Quote]. BrainyQuote. https://www.brainyquote.com/quotes/mohsin_hamid_530793

Harvard University. (2022, October 14). *8 time management tips for students.* https://summer.harvard.edu/blog/8-time-management-tips-for-students/

Headspace. (n.d.). *How gratitude can increase positivity.* https://organizations.headspace.com/blog/how-gratitude-can-increase-positivity

Hirschfeld, M. (2024, April 22). *What is reflective listening? The key to deeper connections and better communication.* Holding Hope Marriage & Family Therapy. https://holdinghopemft.com/what-is-reflective-listening-the-key-to-deeper-connections-and-better-communication/

Imbastoni, G. (2023, May 5). *Create a personal vision statement and change your life.* BetterUp. https://www.betterup.com/blog/create-a-personal-vision-statement

Jaffe, C. A. (n.d.). *It's not your salary that makes you rich, it's your spending habits* [Quote]. Quote Sanity. https://quotesanity.com/living-below-your-means-quotes/

James, W. (n.d.). *The greatest weapon against stress is our ability to choose one thought over another* [Quote]. AZ Quotes. https://www.azquotes.com/quote/574388

Kaiser Permanente. (2023, December 29). *The physical and mental benefits of exercise for teens.* My Doctor Online. https://mydoctor.kaiserpermanente.org/mas/news/the-physical-and-mental-benefits-of-exercise-for-teens-2325553

Kassem, S. (n.d.). *Doubt kills more dreams than failure ever will* [Quote]. The Random Vibez. https://www.therandomvibez.com/self-doubt-quotes/

Kennedy, J. F. (n.d.). *Efforts and courage are not enough without purpose and direction* [Quote]. BrainyQuote. https://www.brainyquote.com/quotes/john_f_kennedy_164001

Klein, D., & Madden, H. (2024, December 12). *How to improve body language to send the right message.* wikiHow. https://www.wikihow.com/Communicate-With-Body-Language

Le Cunff, A.-L. (2020, February 19). *Constructive criticism: How to give and receive feedback.* Ness Labs. https://nesslabs.com/constructive-criticism-give-receive-feedback

Levison, A. (n.d.). *Building a strong support system: How to surround yourself with positive people.* Neurofeedback & Counseling Center. https://www.neuroandcounselingcenter.com/single-post/building-strong-support-system

Life Coach Training. (n.d.). *Resilience and mental toughness: Case studies and success stories.* https://lifecoachtraining.co/resilience-and-mental-toughness-case-studies-and-success-stories/

Lin, C. (2023, November 16). *Tools to protect your privacy on social media*. NetChoice. https://netchoice.org/tools-to-protect-your-privacy-on-social-media/

LinkedIn. (n.d.). *How can you use role-play to resolve conflicts?*. https://www.linkedin.com/advice/0/how-can-you-use-role-play-resolve-conflicts-skills-linguistics-ub9wf

Lohmann, R. C. (2015, December 23). *Top 20 social networking etiquette tips for teens. Psychology Today*. https://www.psychologytoday.com/us/blog/teen-angst/201512/top-20-social-networking-etiquette-tips-teens

Martins, J. (2024, February 25). *Are you time blocking your calendar? Here's why you should start now*. Asana. https://asana.com/resources/what-is-time-blocking

Modern Hikes. (2024, July 25). *Exploring the benefits of mindfulness and meditation*. https://www.modernhikes.com/exploring-the-benefits-of-mindfulness-and-meditation/

My Deep Meditation. (n.d.). *The art of listening: Tips for improving communication with your child*. http://mydeepmeditation.com/the-art-of-listening-tips-for-improving-communication-with-your-child/

My Kids Vision. (n.d.). *Screen time in teenagers: How can we manage it?* https://www.mykidsvision.org/knowledge-centre/screen-time-in-teenagers-how-can-we-manage-it

Nunez, K. (2020, August 10). *Progressive muscle relaxation: Benefits, how-to, technique*. Healthline. https://www.healthline.com/health/progressive-muscle-relaxation

The Orion School. (n.d.). *Conflict resolution strategies: Navigating disagreements in student relationships*. https://theorionschool.org/blog/student-conflict-resolution-strategies-guide

Preston, E. (2022, December 6). *Tips to overcome procrastination in school*. Connections Academy. https://www.connectionsacademy.com/support/resources/article/tips-to-overcome-procrastination-in-school/

Purdue Global. (2022, May 13). *The student's guide to SMART goals*. https://www.purdueglobal.edu/blog/student-life/smart-goals-for-students/

Ridley, C., & Crosby, J. (2023, July 27). *How to gain someone's trust back: Manageable steps for rebuilding security and stability in relationships*. Thriveworks. https://thriveworks.com/help-with/relationships/how-to-gain-trust-back/

Rivas-Drake, D., Markstrom, C., Syed, M., Lee, R. M., Umaña-Taylor, A. J., Yip, T., Seaton, E. K., Quintana, S., Schwartz, S. J., & French, S. (2014). *Ethnic and racial identity in adolescence: Implications for psychosocial, academic, and health outcomes. Child Development*, 85(1), 40–57. https://srcd.onlinelibrary.wiley.com/doi/10.1111/cdev.12200

Rodrigues, R. I., Lopes, P., & Varela, M. (2021). *Factors affecting impulse buying behavior of consumers*. Frontiers in Psychology, 12, Article 697080. https://doi.org/10.3389/fpsyg.2021.697080

RuPaul. (n.d.). *If you can't love yourself, how in the hell are you gonna love somebody else?* [Quote]. *RuPaul's Drag Race.* World of Wonder Productions.

Schwarz, N. (n.d.). *How to teach growth mindset to teens.* Big Life Journal. https://biglifejournal.com/blogs/blog/teaching-teens-growth-mindset

Scroggs, L. (n.d.). *The Pomodoro Technique — Why it works & how to do it.* Todoist. https://todoist.com/productivity-methods/pomodoro-technique

StoryCorps. (n.d.). *Lesson: The power of active listening.* https://storycorps.org/discover/education/lesson-the-power-of-active-listening/

Tilly's Life Center. (2022, October 25). *The mental health benefits of journaling for teens.* https://tillyslifecenter.org/2022/10/25/journaling-for-teens-mental-health-resources/

Troly-Curtin, M. (1912). *Phrynette Married.* Grant Richards Ltd.

UC Davis Health. (2022, August 3). *How blue light affects your eyes, sleep, and health.* Cultivating Health Blog. https://health.ucdavis.edu/blog/cultivating-health/blue-light-effects-on-your-eyes-sleep-and-health/2022/08

University at Buffalo School of Social Work. (n.d.). *Developing your support system.* University at Buffalo. https://socialwork.buffalo.edu/resources/self-care-starter-kit/additional-self-care-resources/developing-your-support-system.html

Vallejo, M. (2023, October 6). *Time management for teens: Challenges, strategies, and tips.* Mental Health Center Kids. https://mentalhealthcenterkids.com/blogs/articles/time-management-for-teens

Van Edwards, V. (2024, July 2). *Mirroring body language: 4 steps to successfully mirror others.* Science of People. https://www.scienceofpeople.com/mirroring/

Versace, D. (n.d.). *Creativity comes from a conflict of ideas* [Quote]. AZ Quotes. https://www.azquotes.com/quote/302491

WebMD. (2021, August 25). *How to break up with a toxic friend.* https://www.webmd.com/balance/features/toxic-friends-less-friend-more-foe

Wells, I. (2024, September 28). *Shifting perspectives with empathy mapping and role-playing.* The Core Collaborative. https://thecorecollaborative.com/shifting-perspectives-with-empathy-mapping-and-role-playing/

West, M. (2022, April 21). *What to know about guided imagery.* Medical News Today. https://www.medicalnewstoday.com/articles/guided-imagery

Withe, M. (2024, January 15). *18 mindfulness activities for teens and students.* Medical News Today. https://www.medicalnewstoday.com/articles/mindfulness-activities-for-teens

Yang, A. (2023, February 10). *Passion projects for high school students: Why they're important and how to get started.* Polygence. https://www.polygence.org/blog/passion-projects-for-high-school-students-guide

Youth.gov. (n.d.). *Career exploration and skill development.* https://youth.gov/youth-topics/youth-employment/career-exploration-and-skill-development

Youth Villages. (2023, May 11). *5 ways to teach your teens healthy boundaries.* https://youthvillages.org/5-ways-to-teach-your-teens-healthy-boundaries/